ADVENTURES IN
SPACE

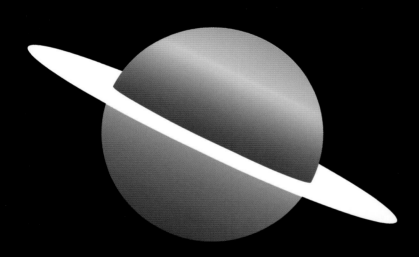

SIMON TYLER

PAVILION

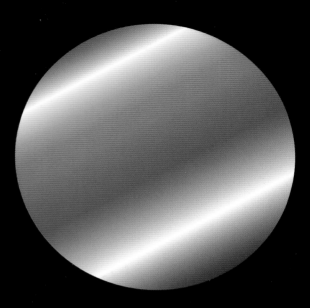
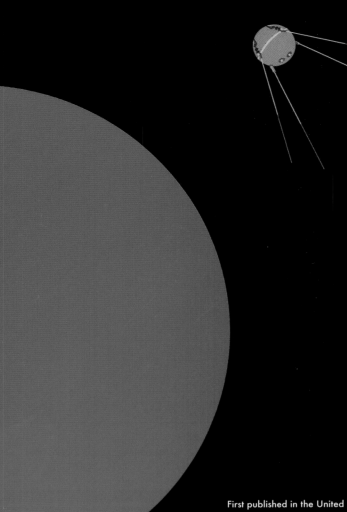

First published in the United Kingdom in 2018 by
Pavilion Children's Books
43 Great Ormond Street
London
WC1N 3HZ

An imprint of Pavilion Books Limited.

Publisher and Editor: Neil Dunnicliffe
Assistant Editor: Hattie Grylls
Art Director: Anna Lubecka

ISBN: 9781843653745

A CIP catalogue record for this book is available from the British Library.

10 9 8 7 6 5 4 3 2 1

Reproduction by Rival Colour UK

Printed by Leefung Printing Ltd, China

This book can be ordered directly from the publisher online
at www.pavilionbooks.com, or try your local bookshop.

CONTENTS

INTRODUCTION

Welcome to the amazing world of space

ver since the first humans gazed up into the night sky we, as a species, h
ascinated by the stars, the planets, the universe and our place within it.

Over the centuries, our knowledge and understanding of the science of sp
rown by an amazing extent. We are now able to recognise distant plane
ravitational waves from black holes, and monitor near-Earth objects that r
ollision course with our own planet.

We have also created vehicles that have allowed humans to travel into spc
arth and explore the Moon. We have constructed space stations that allo
o live in space for prolonged periods. And we have developed new techr
vhich could allow us to venture further, beyond the Moon, to explore othe

he aim of this book is to give you a good understanding of the science of
ur relationship with the Sun and the other planets in the Solar System, ou
he Milky Way, and the universe as a whole. The first section of the book f
he exploration of space from Earth – the science of astronomy – and how
eveloped our understanding of the universe.

he second section investigates space travel, and how we have used spac
robes to explore physically the nature of our neighbouring Moon and loc
h parts of this book you may find some scientific terms that you are unfam
he first time these are used they are highlighted in CAPITALS, and all of th
nd phrases are explained in the glossary at the end of the book

VOYAGER 1

Country: USA
Launched: 5 September 1977
Length: 17 m
Width: 6.4 m
Height: 2.9 m
Weight: 825 kg

A space probe launched by NASA in
September 1977, Voyager 1 is now over 20
billion kilometres from Earth. It is the most
distant man-made object in the universe.

During its 40-year-long mission, it
has passed through the asteroid belt,
performed flybys of Saturn and Jupiter,
and travelled into interstellar space. It is
powered by three electrical generators
fuelled by radioactive plutonium. These
will run out of power in 2025.

ASTRONOMY

What is astronomy? It is the name we use to describe the science of space.

Observation of the night sky is a fundamental aspect of astronomy. Originally this was done with the naked eye. In the 17th century the telescope was invented, which allowed astronomers to see much further into space, and observe the planets in more detail. Since then, scientists have built bigger and bigger telescopes, including ones which can 'see' things that our eyes can't, like x-rays, infrared and even radio waves. We have even launched telescopes into space!

Astronomers use maths to calculate and describe the movement of planets, stars and other bodies through space. The same techniques can be used by ASTRONAUTS to navigate their spacecraft. If you want to become an astronaut one day, you need to work hard in maths lessons!

Astronomers use the theories of physics to understand the mechanics and structure of the universe. The astronomical discoveries of the Renaissance provided laws which offer very accurate descriptions of how bodies (e.g. planets) in space interact with each other. Since then, advances in physics have allowed us to explain other phenomena. We now know how stars such as the Sun create both energy and chemical elements in their cores. We have proved the existence of BLACK HOLES and gravitational waves, and confirmed these discoveries by observation.

Astronomers use the science of chemistry to discover what distant bodies are made of. By analysing observations from radio telescopes, they can detect the presence of different chemical elements and molecules in the far reaches of space.

Because of the hard work performed by astronomers and scientists over the centuries, we now possess an amazing degree of knowledge and understanding of the nature and history of the universe.

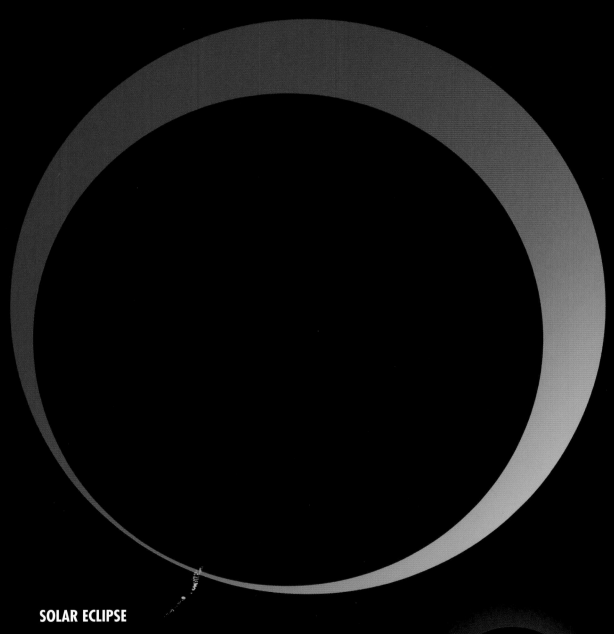

SOLAR ECLIPSE

Eclipses of the Sun are some of the most dramatic astronomical phenomena that can be viewed from Earth.

When the Moon passes between the Earth and the Sun, it casts a shadow which obscures our view of the Sun. Most solar eclipses are partial (large illustration above), when the Sun and Moon are not in line with the Earth, and so the Moon only obscures part of the Sun.

When they are lined up and the Moon obscures the whole of the Sun, it is known as a total eclipse (right). A total eclipse results in a dark sky, and reveals the faint CORONA which surrounds the sun.

EARLY ASTRONOMY

Humans have studied the stars and planets since the beginning of human history. Ancient peoples around the world believed that these things in the sky – CELESTIAL BODIES – were controlled by the gods and spirits, and they also controlled the seasons and weather on Earth. Around 5300 years ago the ancient Mesopotamians were one of the first civilisations to separate the science of astronomy from religious ASTROLOGY. They charted the positions of stars in the sky, creating the first star charts.

Claudius Ptolemy was a Greco-Roman scientist, who lived in the Egyptian city of Alexandria between 100 and 170 CE. He used the Mesopotamian star charts, along with his own observations and those of an earlier Greek scientist, Hipparchus, to develop a complete theory of the stars and planets. Such a theory is known as a COSMOLOGY, and his treatise was called the Almagest. Ptolemy's view was that the Earth was in the centre of the universe, and so his cosmology is called GEOCENTRIC.

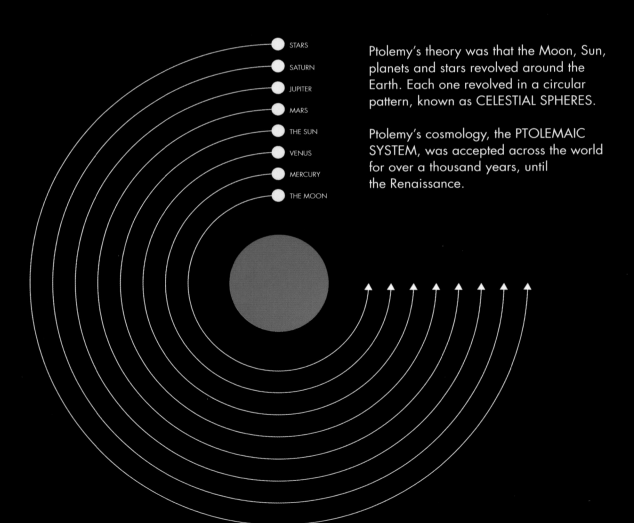

STARS
SATURN
JUPITER
MARS
THE SUN
VENUS
MERCURY
THE MOON

Ptolemy's theory was that the Moon, Sun, planets and stars revolved around the Earth. Each one revolved in a circular pattern, known as CELESTIAL SPHERES.

Ptolemy's cosmology, the PTOLEMAIC SYSTEM, was accepted across the world for over a thousand years, until the Renaissance.

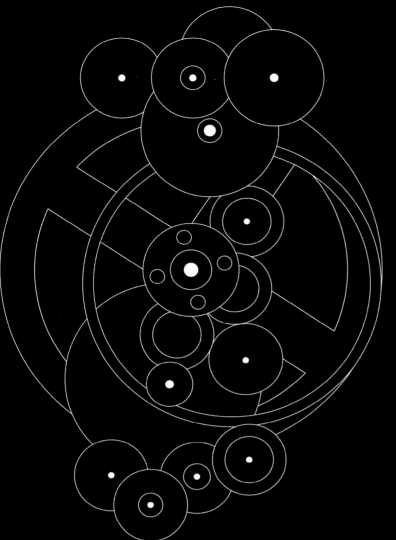

The Antikythera mechanism (left) was an early Greek mechanical computing device. Discovered in an ancient shipwreck off the coast of the island of Antikythera, it is thought to date from around 100 BCE.

The device used a very complicated system of gears and dials to predict the positions of the Moon and Sun in the night sky, and also to predict eclipses.

Born around 350 CE, Hypatia of Alexandria was the head of the great Alexandrian school and an important mathematician and astronomer. As well as teaching and editing the works of Ptolemy, Plato and Aristotle, she used her own observations to produce detailed tables of celestial phenomena, especially equinoxes. Predicting equinox dates was important to the Greeks as they were used in calendars and also as festivals.

Hypatia is one of the earliest scientists known to have used a plane astrolabe (right) – a tool used to identify and measure the position of stars and planets in the sky. She is known to have constructed astrolabes herself.

THE BOOK OF FIXED STARS

Abd al-Rahman al-Sufi, also known as Azophi, was an Abbasid astronomer who lived between 903 and 986 CE in Isfahan (in modern day Iran). He was one of the most important Islamic astronomers, and studied Ptolemy's findings carefully.

His own work was called *The Book of Fixed Stars*. It included precise drawings of the constellations, such as Cepheus (below left), Virgo (left) and Ursa Major (below right). He was also the first person to observe and record other galaxies, including the Andromeda Galaxy and the Large Magellanic Cloud.

THE RENAISSANCE

In the middle of the 14th century there was a scientific revolution in Europe. Many of the ancient scientific writings, which had been lost for many years, were rediscovered and the knowledge they contained helped the scientists and astronomers of the day to develop new ideas and theories about the nature of science and space.

Ptolemy's geocentric system remained unchallenged until the 15th century. Nicolaus Copernicus, who lived between 1473 and 1543 in Royal Prussia (now Poland), began to develop a new system based on his observations of the planets and their motions. His theory was called *On the Revolutions of the Heavenly Spheres*, which he presented in 1543 – the year he died.

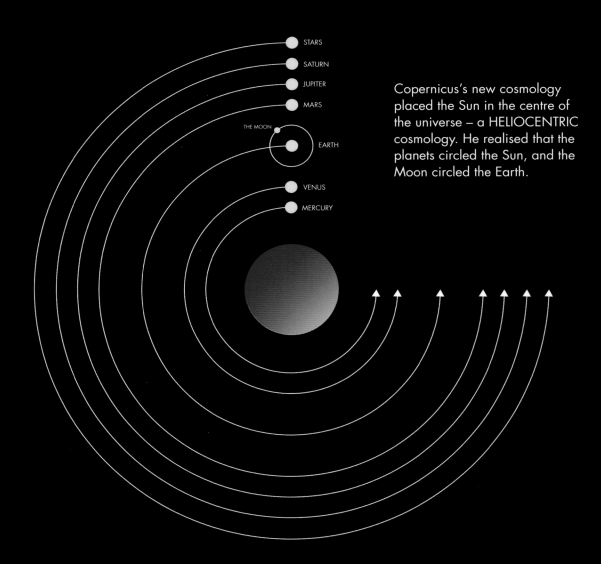

STARS
SATURN
JUPITER
MARS
THE MOON
EARTH
VENUS
MERCURY

Copernicus's new cosmology placed the Sun in the centre of the universe – a HELIOCENTRIC cosmology. He realised that the planets circled the Sun, and the Moon circled the Earth.

He also realised that the stars are much further away than the distance between the Sun and the Earth.

Sophia Brahe (1556–1643) and her brother Tycho advanced the precision of celestial observations by improving the accuracy of astronomical instruments, although they were still reliant on using the naked eye.

They tried to combine Copernicus's theory with that of Ptolemy. They realised that the stars and planets circled the Sun, but believed that the Moon and the Sun circled the Earth. Whilst they were mistaken, their accurate observations and calculations were still very useful for later astronomers.

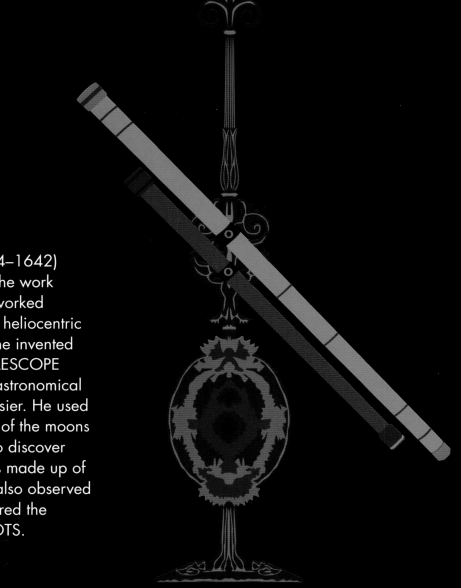

Galileo Galilei (1564–1642) believed strongly in the work of Copernicus, and worked tirelessly to prove his heliocentric theory. In doing so, he invented the REFRACTING TELESCOPE (right), which made astronomical observation much easier. He used this to discover three of the moons of Jupiter, and also to discover that the Milky Way is made up of millions of stars. He also observed the Sun, and discovered the existence of SUNSPOTS.

PLANETARY MOTION

In the 17th century, the German astronomer Johannes Kepler developed the Copernican system further. He studied the motion of the planets in greater detail and realised that the paths they followed around the Sun were not circular, as had been previously thought.

Between 1609 and 1619 Kepler produced his Laws of Planetary Motion, which remain accurate tools for calculating the orbits of planets around a much bigger object such as the Sun. Although Kepler could only observe the planets as far out as Jupiter and Saturn, his laws work perfectly to describe Uranus and Neptune too.

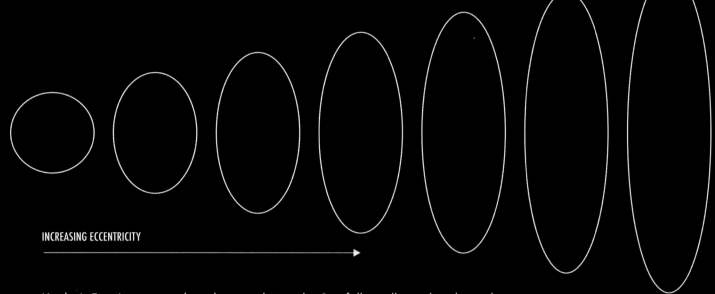

INCREASING ECCENTRICITY

Kepler's First Law states that planets orbiting the Sun follow elliptical paths, rather than exact circles as previously thought. A circle is a type of ELLIPSE, and the diagram above shows a series of ellipses, from a circle on the left, stretching into longer ovals. The more stretched out an ellipse is, the more ECCENTRIC it is said to be.

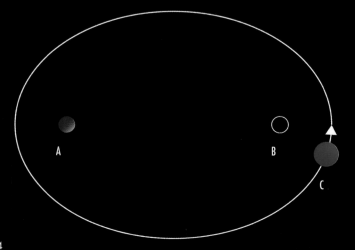

Except for perfect circles, all ellipses have two FOCAL POINTS, or FOCI. Perfect circles have a single focus, in the middle. As ellipses become more eccentric, the foci move closer and closer to the edge.

In the ellipse on the left, the foci are marked A and B.

In planetary orbit systems, the larger body – in this case the Sun – sits at one of the foci, and the smaller body – the Earth (C) in this case – travels around it on an elliptical path.

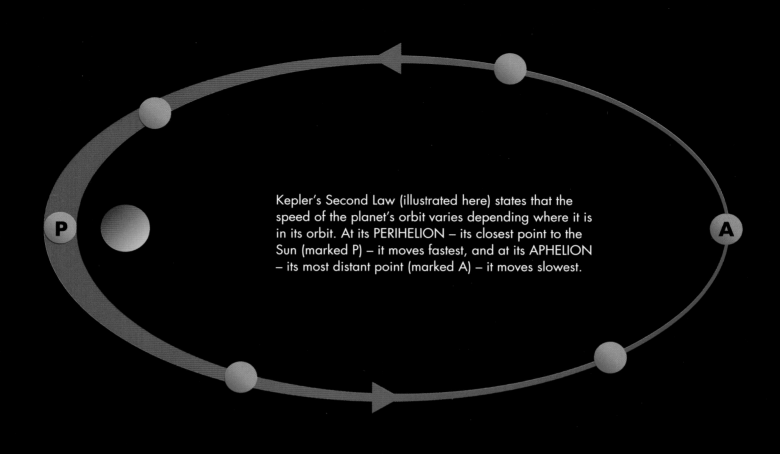

Kepler's Second Law (illustrated here) states that the speed of the planet's orbit varies depending where it is in its orbit. At its PERIHELION – its closest point to the Sun (marked P) – it moves fastest, and at its APHELION – its most distant point (marked A) – it moves slowest.

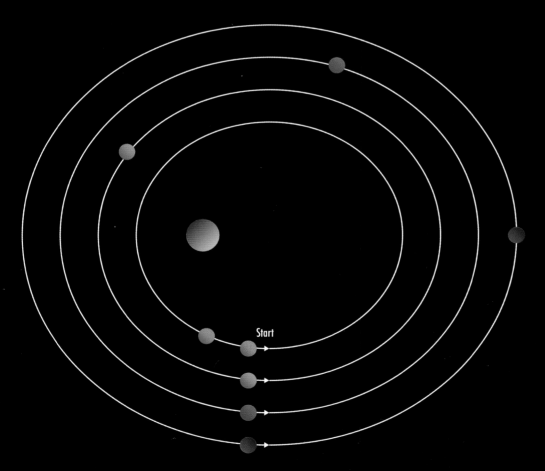

Start

Kepler's Third Law (left) states that the time it takes for a planet to perform one orbital revolution gets greater the further away the planet is from the Sun.

In this diagram, if all the planets begin their orbit at the point marked 'Start', the innermost orbiting planet will have almost finished its orbit while the outermost will have only travelled a quarter of its full orbit.

For example, the Earth takes 1 year to orbit the Sun. In comparison, Neptune, which is much more distant, takes 164 years to complete its orbit around the Sun.

GRAVITY

Johannes Kepler's Laws of Planetary Motion were ground-breaking discoveries which provided the first accurate descriptions of the movement of the planets around the Sun. Later, the British scientist Isaac Newton investigated the forces that he believed caused the planetary motions that Kepler had observed.

Newton's discoveries led him to propose his law of universal gravitation, which he developed when he was 23 years old. He later followed this with his three universal laws of motion. His scientific discoveries were so revolutionary that they would have a lasting influence on astronomy and physics through the centuries after his death and until the present day.

Isaac Newton described GRAVITY as a force of attraction that is generated by all objects with mass, from the smallest atom to the largest star.

He showed that the gravitational force between a pair of objects depends on the total mass of the two objects, and the distance between them. The greater the total mass, the greater the force of attraction. The more distant the objects, the smaller the force of attraction. In the diagram on the right, the forces on each of the objects (A and B) are equal. If the distance between them (C) is greater, the forces are smaller.

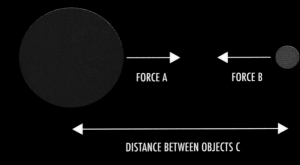

FORCE A   FORCE B

DISTANCE BETWEEN OBJECTS C

Although every object is attracted to every other object, in practice the forces between them are almost imperceptible because the masses are small. Gravity is much more noticeable when there is a large mass. For example, everything on Earth is dominated by the effects of the Earth's own gravity.

Because the Moon is much less massive than the Earth, the effects of gravity on the Moon's surface are much smaller. As you can see in the diagram on the right, the gravitational force on the smaller Moon is 0.16 times that experienced on the larger Earth.

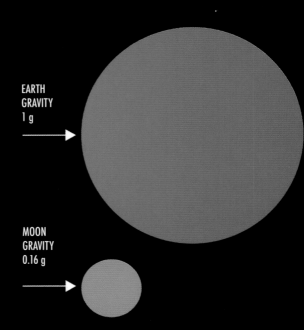

EARTH GRAVITY 1 g

MOON GRAVITY 0.16 g

MOTION

Newton presented his laws of motion in 1686, in his book *Principia Mathematica Philosophiae Naturalis* (The Mathematical Principals of Natural Philosophy). These laws describe and predict the way in which everything in the universe moves and interacts as the result of gravitational attraction. Although Albert Einstein's theory of relativity has since superseded the theories of the *Principia*, in practice Newton's theories are more than adequate for explaining all but the most extreme astronomical situations.

Newton's First Law of Motion states that any object in motion or at rest will remain so, unless a force acts on it. For example, once a space probe such as Cassini (right) has escaped the influence of Earth, it will continue coasting through space until either its engine is restarted or it enters the influence of another massive object, such as another planet.

CASSINI SPACE PROBE

The Second Law of Motion states that the speed of an object changes when a force acts on it. The change of speed is known as ACCELERATION. The acceleration depends on the mass of the object and the amount of force acting on it. For example, a small, satellite-carrying rocket such as the 1960s British Black Arrow (left) requires a much smaller propulsive thrust to accelerate than a very large manned spacecraft such as Gemini-Titan.

BLACK ARROW
THRUST: 68.2 kN

GEMINI-TITAN
THRUST: 1,913 kN

The Third Law of Motion states that whenever a force acts on an object, there is an equal and opposite reaction. For example, when a rocket fires its engine the fiery hot thrust A moves one way, and the rocket itself moves in the opposite direction B.

ROCKET MOTION B

THRUST A

THE SOLAR SYSTEM

The Solar System is the area of space in which our planet – the Earth – and our neighbouring planets orbit our nearest star – the Sun.

The influence of the Sun extends far out into space, much further than the most distant planet. We now know that there are thousands of other objects orbiting the Sun. These include asteroids, dwarf planets, comets and huge clouds of icy fragments.

The Solar System is a huge and complex place!

The four innermost planets of the Solar System are Earth, Mars, Venus and Mercury.

THE SUN

The Sun is the star at the centre of the Solar System. It is by far the largest and most massive object in the Solar System, with a radius over one hundred times that of the Earth, and a mass 330,000 times that of the Earth. The vast size of the Sun is evident when compared with that of the Earth, as viewed on the left.

The mass of the Sun makes up 99.86% of the total mass of the entire Solar System. This huge, concentrated mass has an effect on every single object deep into outer space, due to the force of gravity. Because the Sun is so much bigger than everything nearby, it totally dominates the Solar System, and the orbits of the planets (and other celestial bodies) are caused by its gravity.

Nuclear reactions within the interior of the Sun produce colossal amounts of energy. This energy is released in the form of radiation, including heat and light, without which life would not exist on Earth.

The Sun is 4.6 billion years old. It contains enough fuel to remain stable for more than another 5 billion years. After that, it will begin to enter the final, violent stages of its lifespan.

INSIDE THE SUN

The core of the Sun is a sphere of very hot, high density and high pressure matter, called PLASMA. Within the core, hydrogen atoms join together to form helium in a process called nuclear fusion. In this reaction, a proportion of matter is converted into pure energy. The heat involved is huge – the core reaches temperatures of over 15 million degrees.

Above the core is a layer known as the RADIATION ZONE, where energy moves very gradually outwards. It takes over 170,000 years for energy to travel across the radiation zone.

Above the radiation zone is the CONVECTION ZONE, within which solar matter and energy move much more rapidly. Plasma currents transport heat from the base of the convection zone to the surface of the Sun, where they transmit their heat, cool, and sink back down again.

The boundary between the two zones is called the TACHOCLINE. The interaction of the two works like a dynamo, generating and amplifying huge magnetic forces.

The visible outer surface of the Sun is known as the PHOTOSPHERE. The Sun's heat and light energy is transmitted into space from the photosphere.

PHOTOSPHERE

CONVECTION ZONE

TACHOCLINE

RADIATION ZONE

CORE

OUTSIDE THE SUN

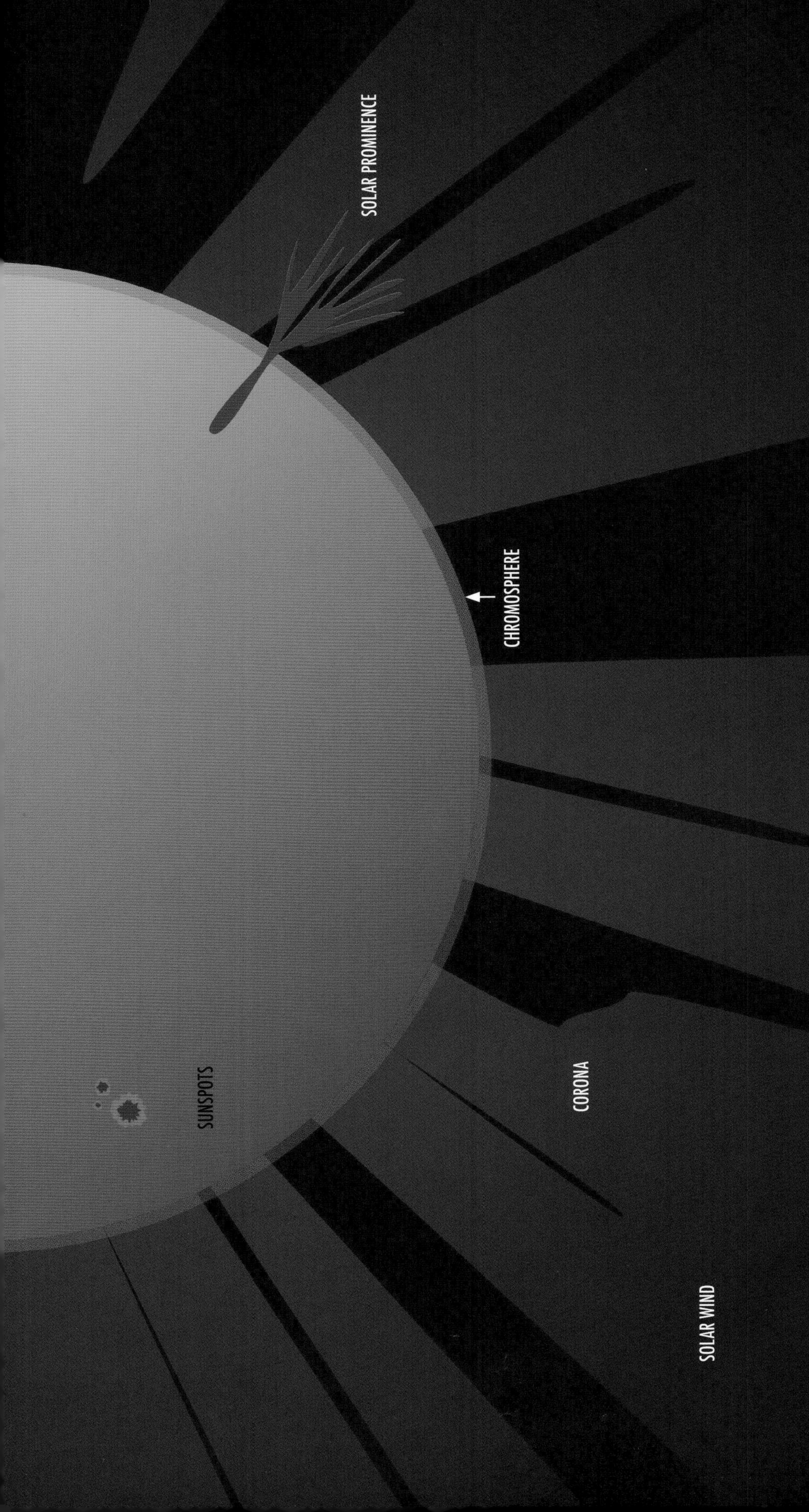

SOLAR PROMINENCE

CHROMOSPHERE

SUNSPOTS

CORONA

SOLAR WIND

The layer above the photosphere is known as the CHROMOSPHERE. This layer extends approximately 2,000 km from the photosphere, and curiously gets hotter at its outermost edge.

SOLAR PROMINENCES are high energy releases of plasma from the Sun's surface.

SUNSPOTS are highly magnetic areas on the surface of the Sun. Their magnetic field causes the Sun's surface to reduce in temperature. The lower temperature means the area appears darker than the surrounding photosphere.

The CORONA is a very high temperature layer of plasma that extends out into space. Its position and thickness depend on activity on the Sun's surface.

The SOLAR WIND is made up of plasma that flows from the corona, away from the Sun, beyond the planets, to the edge of the Solar System.

EARTH
DISTANCE FROM SUN: 149,598,023 km
TIME LIGHT TAKES TO REACH IT: 8 min 20 sec

PLUTO
DISTANCE FROM SUN: 5,906,119,999 km
TIME LIGHT TAKES TO REACH IT: 5 hours 30 min

HELIOPAUSE - THE EDGE OF THE
SUN'S SPHERE OF INFLUENCE
DISTANCE FROM SUN: 18,000,000,000 km
TIME LIGHT TAKES TO REACH IT: 16 hours 40 min

THE NEAREST STAR - PROXIMA CENTURI
DISTANCE FROM SUN: 40,208,000,000,000 km
TIME LIGHT TAKES TO REACH IT: 4.5 years

THE FAR EDGE OF OUR GALAXY - THE MILKY WAY
DISTANCE FROM SUN: 709,600,000,000,000,000 km
TIME LIGHT TAKES TO REACH IT: 75,000 years

THE SPEED OF LIGHT

The speed of light is one of the most important numbers in science. Known as c, its exact value is 299,792,458 metres per second. It is the speed that tiny massless particles and fields travel in the vacuum of space.

Light is made up of particles called PHOTONS. A photon released from the Sun will take approximately 498 seconds, or 8 minutes and 20 seconds, to reach the retina of your eye, when you see it as light.

Light travels amazingly fast, but the universe is so enormous that it actually takes light a very long time to travel between stars and galaxies. This diagram compares the time it takes light to travel between the centre of the Solar System and various other places in the universe.

THE NEAREST FULL-SIZE GALAXY – ANDROMEDA
DISTANCE FROM SUN: 23,650,000,000,000,000,000 km
TIME LIGHT TAKES TO REACH IT: 2,500,000 years

THE MOST DISTANT OBSERVED GALAXY – EGS8p7
DISTANCE FROM SUN: 124,880,000,000,000,000,000,000 km
TIME LIGHT TAKES TO REACH IT: 13,200,000,000 years

THE EDGE OF THE OBSERVABLE UNIVERSE
DISTANCE FROM SUN: 440,000,000,000,000,000,000,000 km
TIME LIGHT TAKES TO REACH IT: 46,000,000,000 years

A RED GIANT

In 5 billion years time the Sun will begin to expand into a RED GIANT.

On the right, you can compare the current size of the Sun with its final red giant size.

Red giants are stars which have used up all the hydrogen in their core. When this runs out, the outward force of energy from the core stops, and then gravity causes the core to squash down. This squashing increases the temperature of the core.

The increased temperature sets off fusion reactions in the upper layers of the star, where some hydrogen remains. This produces an outward force of energy but, unlike the massive core, these layers are not as dense, and the force of energy is not balanced with gravity, so the star begins to expand greatly.

The hugely increased surface area of the star means that it becomes much brighter – its LUMINOSITY has increased. But the temperature at the surface is at a lower temperature now, so the colour shifts to red.

When the Sun becomes a red giant it will engulf the planets Mercury and Venus, and almost certainly Earth, before finally transforming into a WHITE DWARF.

Current radius: 695,700 km

Red giant radius: 300,000,000 km

MERCURY

VENUS

EARTH

MARS

CERES

ASTEROID BELT

JUPITER

THE INNER SOLAR SYSTEM

Millions of objects are in orbit around the Sun, but only eight of these objects are classed as planets. These are the terrestrial planets Mercury, Venus, Earth and Mars, and the giant planets Jupiter, Saturn, Uranus and Neptune.

The terrestrial planets are mainly made up of rock and metal. Beyond the orbit of Mars lies the ASTEROID BELT, which is formed of millions of rock and metal particles. The dwarf planet Ceres is also found here.

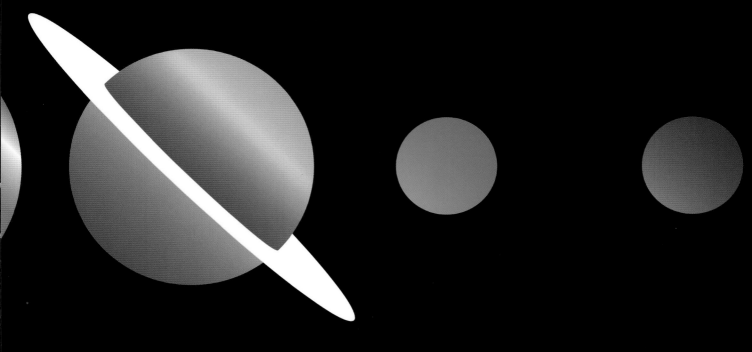

Jupiter and Saturn are gas giants, predominantly made up of hydrogen and helium. The ice giants, Uranus and Neptune, are made up of frozen methane, ammonia and water.

All these planets rotate around the Sun in roughly circular orbits, and in very nearly the same plane, both of which have helped us understand how the Solar System was formed.

SATURN

URANUS

NEPTUNE

THE PLANETS IN DETAIL

MERCURY
Radius: 2,439.7 km
Mass: 3.3011 x 10^{23} kg
Distance from Sun: 46–69 x 10^6 km

The closest planet to the Sun, Mercury, is named after the Roman messenger god. Because of Mercury's small mass, its gravity is not sufficient to maintain much atmosphere, so the temperature at the surface changes between freezing cold and extreme heat. The surface of Mercury is covered with craters, formed by the impacts of asteroids and comets. It is heavily scarred from the effects of space weathering – the constant beating from solar wind particles, meteorites and micrometeorites, and high-energy solar radiation.

VENUS
Radius: 6,051.8 km
Mass: 4.8675 x 10^{24} kg
Distance from Sun: 107–109 x 10^6 km

Named after the Roman god of beauty and love, Venus is a similar size and mass to the Earth. However, it would not make a nice place to live! The atmosphere is mostly made up of carbon dioxide, which acts as a greenhouse gas. Because of this, the temperature on the surface of Venus is approximately 460°C – even hotter than Mercury. Also, the sky is filled with clouds of acid. Viewed from Earth, Venus is the brightest object in the night sky after the Moon.

EARTH
Radius: 6,371.0km
Mass: 5.972 x 10^{24} kg
Distance from Sun: 147–152 x 10^6 km

Unlike the other planets of the Solar System, around 70% of the surface of the Earth is covered with liquid water. Together with the effects of early lifeforms, which transformed a nitrogen and carbon dioxide atmosphere to one rich in oxygen through the process of photosynthesis, life has evolved and thrived on our planet. Oxygen in the upper atmosphere has been converted to ozone, which protects the surface from solar UV radiation, and the atmosphere as a whole works to keep temperatures stable in comparison with the other planets. These factors help explain why the Earth is currently known to be the only body in the Universe that is home to living things.

MARS
Radius: 3,389.5 km
Mass: 6.417 x 10^{23} kg
Distance from Sun: 207–249 x 10^6 km

Mars is the second-smallest planet in the Solar System, and is named after the Roman god of war. Remarkably similar to Earth in some respects, the possibility of discovering life on or in its surface has made Mars a focus for astronomical exploration. Mars has an atmosphere consisting mostly of carbon dioxide, some argon and nitrogen, and traces of oxygen and water.

The surface of Mars has a wide variety of features including large impact craters, volcanoes and canyons. It also has two permanent polar ice caps. The Martian volcano Olympus Mons is the largest known in the Solar System. Mars has two small moons, Phobos and Deimos.

JUPITER
Radius: 69,911 km
Mass: 1.8982 x 10^{27} kg
Distance from Sun: 741–817 x 10^6 km

Jupiter is the largest planet in the Solar System, and is named after the Roman god of the sky. It has 67 known moons, including the four largest Galilean moons (which were discovered by Galileo) Io, Europa, Ganymede and Callisto. Ganymede is the largest moon in the Solar System.

Jupiter is a gas giant – a planet made up of a mixture of gas and liquid matter without a solid surface. It is made up of hydrogen and helium, with traces of methane, water, hydrogen sulfide, and clouds of frozen ammonia crystals.

SATURN
Radius: 58,232 km
Mass: 5.6834×10^{26} kg
Distance from Sun: $1,354–1,513 \times 10^6$ km

The second largest planet in the Solar System after Jupiter, Saturn is named after the Roman god of wealth and farming. Another gas giant, it is mostly made up of hydrogen, with some helium and methane. Its characteristic ring system is made up of water ice and dust particles.

It has 62 known moons, with the largest – Titan – being the second-largest moon in the Solar System after Ganymede.

URANUS
Radius: 25,362 km
Mass: 8.6810×10^{25} kg
Distance from Sun: $2,742–3,008 \times 10^6$ km

Uranus is named after the Greek god of the sky. Previously thought to be a star, it was confirmed as a planet by Sir William Herschel in 1781. Uranus has a small rock and metal core, surrounded by a very thick mantle layer of frozen water, ammonia and methane. Its outer layer comprises a mixture of hydrogen, helium and methane gases.

Uranus has 27 known moons.

NEPTUNE
Radius: 24,622 km
Mass: 1.0243×10^{26} kg
Distance from Sun: $4,460–4,540 \times 10^6$ km

Named after the Roman god of the sea, Neptune has a very similar structure to Uranus, with a rocky core, frozen mantle, and gaseous outer layer. It has very active weather systems, with wind speeds of over 2,000km/h. It is also extremely cold, with temperatures often dropping below −200°C.

Neptune has 14 known moons.

DWARF PLANETS

CERES
Radius: 473 km
Mass: 9.393×10^{20} kg
Distance from Sun: $382–445 \times 10^6$ km

PLUTO
Radius: 1,188 km
Mass: 1.303×10^{22} kg
Distance from Sun: $4.44–7.37 \times 10^9$ km

HAUMEA
Radius: 816 km
Mass: 4.006×10^{21} kg
Distance from Sun: $5.23– 7.7 \times 10^9$ km

MAKEMAKE
Radius: 715 km
Mass: 4.4×10^{21} kg
Distance from Sun: $5.76–7.94 \times 10^9$ km

ERIS
Radius: 1,163 km
Mass: 1.66×10^{22} kg
Distance from Sun: $5.72–14.6 \times 10^9$ km

THE OUTER
SOLAR
SYSTEM

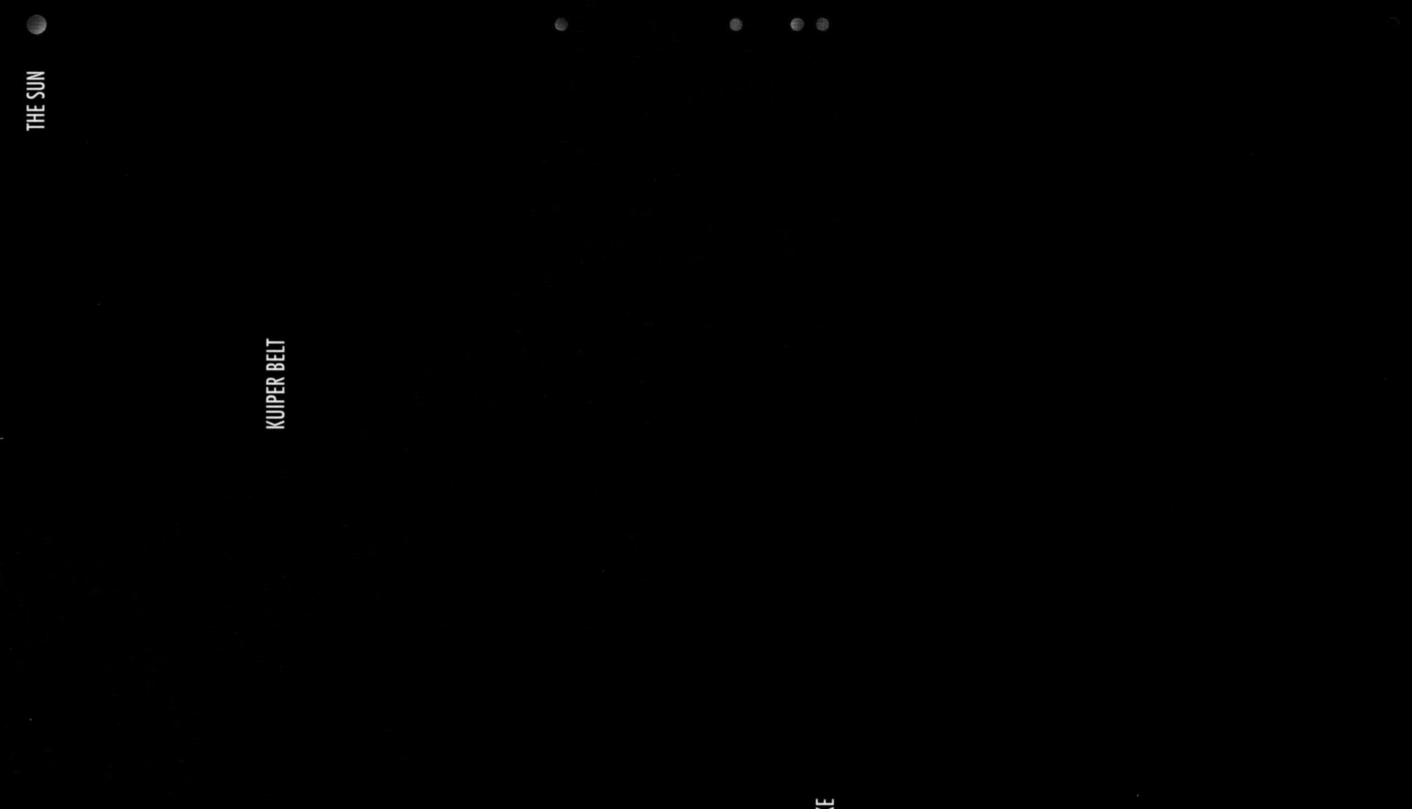

THE SUN

KUIPER BELT

NEPTUNE

PLUTO

HAUMEA
MAKEMAKE

ERIS

Beyond Neptune lies an area of space known as the KUIPER BELT. Like the asteroid belt, this is made up of millions of small objects orbiting the Sun in a defined area. Unlike the asteroid belt, the Kuiper belt objects are icy, consisting of mainly frozen gases and water.

The Kuiper belt is also home to dwarf planets, including Pluto, Makemake and Haumea. The dwarf planet Eris lies beyond the Kuiper belt.

Beyond Eris lies a gigantic cloud of small icy particles, known as the OORT CLOUD. Thought to be the birthplace of comets, the Oort cloud is the most distant part of the Solar System. Beyond that lies interstellar space.

OORT CLOUD
$7,500-30,000 \times 10^9$
km from centre of
solar system

COMETS

A particularly spectacular type of space object visible from Earth with the naked eye, comets were known to ancient humans and were a source of great wonder. They are small icy bodies which orbit the Sun on highly elliptical orbits. When they pass close to the Sun, they heat up and the gases and dust they produce form incredibly long tails in the night sky.

The solid part of a comet is known as the NUCLEUS. This is a small body, between a few hundred metres to 30km in diameter. It is made up of a mixture of rock, dust, and frozen gases, like a dirty snowball.

In 2014 the ESA Rosetta mission successfully landed a lander, called Phillae, on the nucleus of comet 67P/Churyumov-Gerasimenko.

As the comet nears the sun it warms up, and the frozen gases boil to form a very thin atmosphere around the nucleus. This is called a COMA. Although the nucleus is tiny, the coma can reach a huge size, even as large as the Sun itself.

The pressure of the solar wind forces the gases and particles released by the heating comet into two long streams, known as tails. They are even bigger than the coma, and can reach 3 times the distance between the Earth and the Sun. The dust tail points closer to the path the comet has taken. The gas tail points directly away from the Sun.

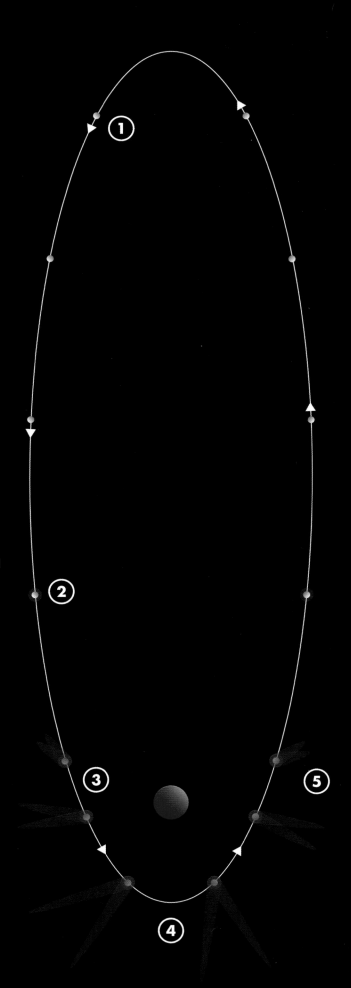

1 While the comet is located towards its aphelion, it remains a small lump of dust, rock and frozen gas. In this state comets are usually dark in colour and don't reflect much light. As such, it is very hard to detect them from Earth.

2 As the comet moves closer to the Sun, the coma begins to form. The coma gives the comet a fuzzy appearance, which helps astronomers to identify the comet. The fuzziness helps to distinguish the comet from background stars.

3 The comet begins to form its distinctive tails. These get longer as the comet moves towards its perihelion.

4 As the comet passes its perihelion, the tails reach their maximum length. The gas tail (blue) always points directly away from the Sun. The dust tail (beige) follows a path closer to the one the comet has taken.

5 As the comet moves away from the Sun, its tails gradually reduce in size, until they disappear.

THE MILKY WAY

Our Solar System is located in a galaxy called the MILKY WAY.

Made up of hundreds of millions of stars, it is a giant spiral structure over 100,000 light years in diameter. It rotates in space around its centre. In the very middle, a point known as the GALACTIC CENTRE, is a strange and very massive object. This is called Sagittarius A* and is thought to be a SUPERMASSIVE BLACK HOLE.

The stars that make up the Milky Way are structured into shapes that curve out from the galactic centre. These are known as SPIRAL ARMS.

The Sun and the Solar System are located roughly two thirds of the way out from the galactic centre, on the Orion-Cygnus Arm.

The Solar System, within the Orion-Cygnus Spiral Arm

BIG STARS

Alpha Boötis
Red giant star
Diameter: 25.4x Sun

THE SUN
Diameter: 1,390,000 km

Aldebaran
Orange giant star
Diameter: 43.9x Sun

P Cygni
Luminous blue variable star
Diameter: 76x Sun

Deneb
Blue white supergiant star
Diameter: 203x Sun

UY Scuti
Red supergiant star
Diameter: 1,708x Sun

SMALL STARS

The variety of stars in the universe is immense. The smallest star so far measured is OGLE-TR-122b, a tiny star in the Carina constellation only a little bigger than the planet Jupiter. The largest star ever discovered is UY Scuti in the Scutum constellation. It is 1,700 times larger than the Sun and, in the illustration on the left, at that scale it would be 17 metres wide!

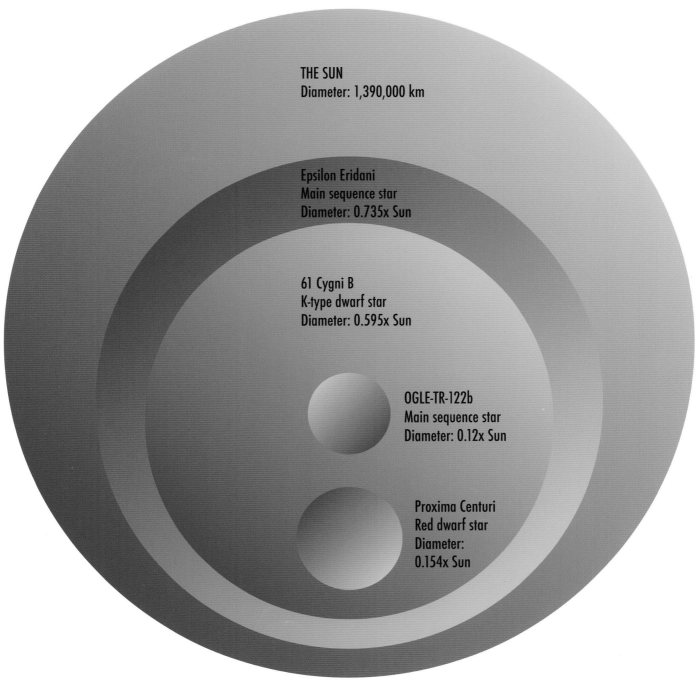

THE SUN
Diameter: 1,390,000 km

Epsilon Eridani
Main sequence star
Diameter: 0.735x Sun

61 Cygni B
K-type dwarf star
Diameter: 0.595x Sun

OGLE-TR-122b
Main sequence star
Diameter: 0.12x Sun

Proxima Centuri
Red dwarf star
Diameter:
0.154x Sun

NEUTRON STARS

When larger stars reach the end of their lives, they sometimes undergo a process whereby their core collapses inwards. In stars with masses between 10 to 25 times the mass of the Sun, these collapsed cores form NEUTRON STARS.

Neutron stars are extremely dense. For example, a piece of neutron star the size of a grain of sand (like the dot below) would have a mass of 38 thousand tons. For comparison, that is more than twice the mass of a US Ohio class ballistic missile submarine. A piece of a neutron star the size of a pea (below right) would have a mass of 118 million tons, which is twenty times the mass of the Great Pyramid of Giza.

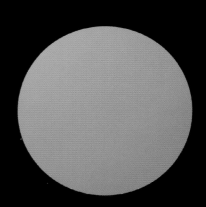

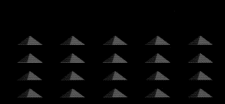

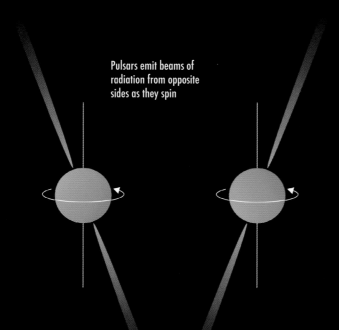

Pulsars emit beams of radiation from opposite sides as they spin

In July 1967 the British astrophysicist Jocelyn Bell Burnell discovered a radio pulse from a distant location in space. She named it Little Green Man (LGM-1), and it was discovered to be a new type of star.

PULSARS (short for pulsating star) are a type of neutron star which emits beams of radiation from opposite sides, and also spins very fast. The beam and the rotation are not lined up, so the beam spins round a path that forms a cone shape.

The pulsar beam is only detected when it points at Earth, and the rotation is regular, so the beam is detected as a very regular pulse.

There is a clock in Gdansk, Poland, which uses a radio telescope tracking six separate pulsars to calculate the time to an extremely high degree of accuracy.

MAGNETARS AND STARQUAKES

Because of their colossal density, neutron stars have huge forces and fields acting within them. One particular type of neutron star exhibits immense magnetic field forces. These are known as MAGNETARS. Magnetars emit large quantities of radiation in the x-ray and gamma ray range of the electromagnetic spectrum.

Over time, magnetars can build up large concentrations of stress in their crusts. Sometimes these stress concentrations are released, in a similar manner to the release of tectonic plate stress on Earth. On Earth, we call these earthquakes. On magnetars, they are known as starquakes.

Starquakes release very large quantities of radiation out into space.

On 27 December 2004, radiation reached Earth from a starquake on a magnetar situated on the other side of the Milky Way, in the constellation of Sagittarius.

Despite the relatively small size of the magnetar, the starquake explosion was probably the most violent and brightest seen in our galaxy since the supernova observed by Kepler in 1604. The starquake lasted 0.1 seconds. In that time, it emitted energy equivalent to that released by the Sun in over 100,000 years!

If magnetar SGR 1806-20 had been closer to Earth, the starquake explosion would have destroyed the Earth's ozone layer and caused mass extinctions.

SGR 1806-20
Diameter: 20 km
Mass: 12.391x Sun (2.46×10^{31} kg)
Distance from Earth: 50,000 ly
Rotation: Every 7.5 sec
Magnetic field: 10^{15}x the Sun

BLACK HOLES

One of the most mysterious phenomena in the universe is another type of super massive entity, which is even more dense than neutron stars. Most black holes are created when very large stars collapse, in a similar process to neutron stars. These are known as stellar black holes.

Unlike neutron stars, the matter making up a black hole has been squeezed down into a much smaller volume at its very centre. This point is known as the SINGULARITY.

This is so dense that its gravity affects not just matter but also light. Within an area around the singularity, known as the EVENT HORIZON, it sucks in everything. This is why black holes appear black, because no light can escape. The path of light passing outside the event horizon is bent, rather like when light passes through a lens. This is known as GRAVITATIONAL LENSING. The picture on the right illustrates the strange curves of light visible around a black hole, which are caused by gravitational lensing.

The size of the event horizon depends on the mass of the black hole, and is known as the SCHWARZSCHILD RADIUS, after the German physicist Karl Schwarzschild. Stellar black holes usually have Schwarzschild radii of between 10–30km.

Over time, black holes can grow by attracting more matter, or combining with other black holes. The very largest, known as supermassive black holes, can reach masses billions of times larger than that of the Sun. These are found in the centre of virtually all galaxies. In the case of the Milky Way, the supermassive black hole is known as Sagittarius A*, and it is 4,000,000 times the mass of the Sun.

As supermassive black holes pull matter towards their centre, discs form around the event horizon. Because of friction, these reach very high temperatures and release huge amounts of radiation, which can be detected with x-ray telescopes.

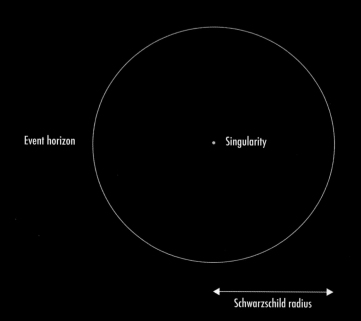

Event horizon

• Singularity

Schwarzschild radius

SPACE TRAVEL

The idea of travelling into space was the long-held dream of many scientists and astronomers over the centuries. However, it wasn't until the 20th century that the development of rocket technology made this dream a real possibility.

The first human-made object that was successfully launched into space was the German V2 rocket (p.66), which reached an altitude of 176 km in June 1944, during testing in World War II. This was a military rocket, designed as a weapon – a ballistic missile. The technology developed by the German rocket engineers would have a huge effect on the future of space exploration.

After the war, the rocket scientists who had developed the V2 continued their work on civilian rockets. Some moved to America, and some went to the Soviet Union (now Russia). An intense rivalry developed between these two superpowers, which was to lead to a SPACE RACE. Both sides desperately wanted to be the first to put a human into space. They would achieve this, and much more!

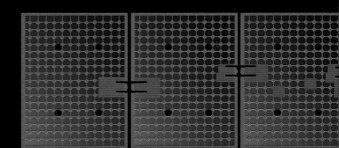

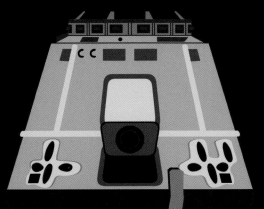

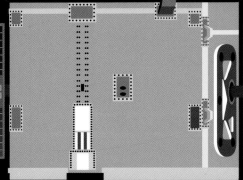

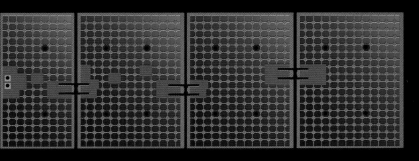

SPACEX DRAGON
Length: 6.1 m
Diameter: 3.7 m
Weight: 4,200 kg

One of the most exciting new spacecraft is the Dragon, developed in California by the private company SpaceX. Dragon was the first spacecraft operated by a private company to successfully return to Earth from orbit.

Dragon is currently used to remotely deliver supplies to the International Space Station.

Dragon is launched on the SpaceX Falcon rocket (p.69). The first stage of the Falcon rocket can return to Earth and land using a combination of parachute and landing thrusters.

BEGINNINGS OF SPACE TRAVEL

Perhaps the most significant single event in the history of space travel was the launch of a diminutive metal sphere, called Sputnik-1. This spacecraft, the name of which means 'fellow traveller' in Russian, was the first artificial satellite ever put into Earth orbit.

On 4 October 1957, an R-7 Semyorka launch vehicle (p.66) blasted off from Baikonur Cosmodrome, in Soviet Kazakhstan. On board was the 83 kilogram metal sphere which was to change history.

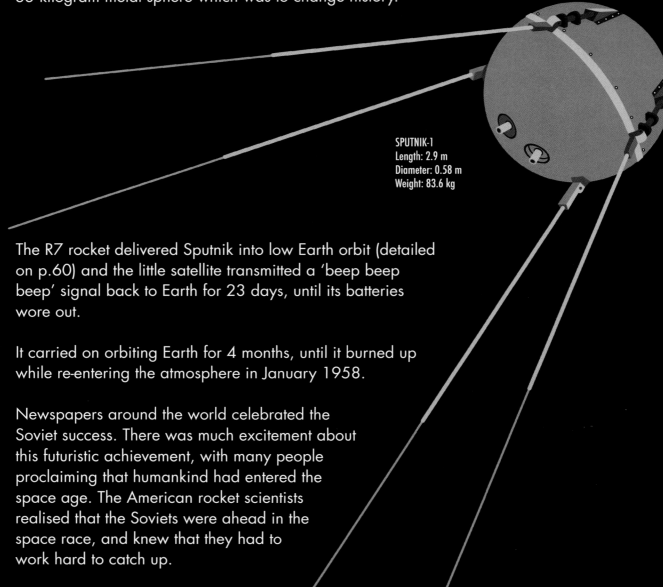

SPUTNIK-1
Length: 2.9 m
Diameter: 0.58 m
Weight: 83.6 kg

The R7 rocket delivered Sputnik into low Earth orbit (detailed on p.60) and the little satellite transmitted a 'beep beep beep' signal back to Earth for 23 days, until its batteries wore out.

It carried on orbiting Earth for 4 months, until it burned up while re-entering the atmosphere in January 1958.

Newspapers around the world celebrated the Soviet success. There was much excitement about this futuristic achievement, with many people proclaiming that humankind had entered the space age. The American rocket scientists realised that the Soviets were ahead in the space race, and knew that they had to work hard to catch up.

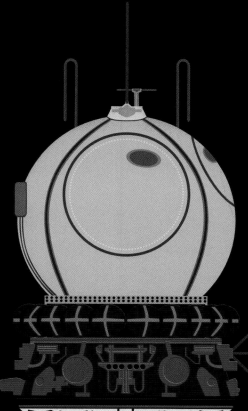

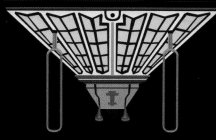

VOSTOK SPACECRAFT
Length: 4.4 m
Diameter: 2.3 m
Weight: 4,730 kg

More satellites were launched, including Sputnik-2, which carried a dog called Laika. The Americans followed this with the launch of their first satellite, Explorer-1 (p.56). However, the next big step came with the launch of the first manned space mission.

Vostok-1 launched from Baikonur on 12 April 1961. A Vostok-K two stage rocket (p.67) carried the Vostok 3KA space capsule (left) into a single orbit around the Earth. The COSMONAUT on board, Yuri Gagarin, became the first human in space.

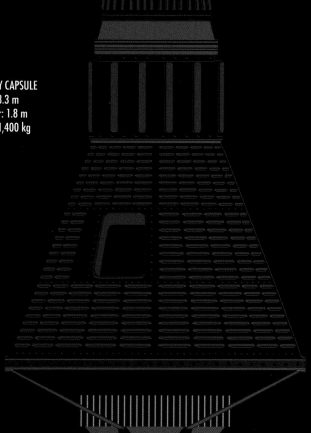

MERCURY CAPSULE
Length: 3.3 m
Diameter: 1.8 m
Weight: 1,400 kg

The first American manned space mission was Mercury-Redstone 3, which launched from Cape Canaveral on 5 May 1961. The Mercury-Redstone rocket (p.66) carried the astronaut Alan Shepard in the Mercury capsule (right) on a sub-orbital trajectory to an altitude of 187.5 km before re-entry and a splashdown in the Atlantic Ocean.

SOYUZ AND GEMINI

The next big step in space travel was the development of longer missions, with more astronauts on board larger spacecraft designed to spend more time in Earth's orbit.

The Russians followed Vostok with another mission called Voskhod, meaning 'ascent'. During these missions, their cosmonauts performed the first spacewalks – known as EVAs (extra-vehicular activities). This involved leaving the safety of the spacecraft through an airlock, and moving around outside in space itself. The early spacesuits they wore were basic and the cosmonauts found it hard to manipulate things because the suits were so stiff.

The Soviets followed Voskhod with their Soyuz series, the first of which launched in April 1967. Soyuz was plagued with technical problems in its early years, and a number of cosmonauts were killed.

However, the design of Soyuz was adjusted and improved, and it became the safest, most reliable, and longest-serving spacecraft ever designed.

The fourth generation of Soyuz is still in operation today and it is the only spacecraft currently able to deliver astronauts to the International Space Station.

SOYUZ 7K-OK CAPSULE
Length: 7.9 m
Diameter: 2.7 m
Weight: 6,500 kg

The Americans followed Mercury with their Project Gemini. The first crewed mission of this new programme launched in 1965.

Gemini used a larger capsule, with room for two astronauts. Using a more powerful Gemini-Titan launch vehicle (p.67), the Gemini missions were much more ambitious, and astronauts performed a wide variety of activities. These included the first American spacewalk, the first successful docking with an unmanned spacecraft, and the record for the highest altitude orbit of Earth.

The main reason behind much of the research and testing conducted by the Gemini astronauts was because American President John F. Kennedy had announced in 1961 that America was aiming to put astronauts on the Moon. This would be a huge undertaking and, to succeed, would require a vast amount of effort, technological development, and bravery.

GEMINI CAPSULE
Length: 5.6 m
Diameter: 3 m
Weight: 3,790 kg

APOLLO

The Apollo programme – the successful series of missions which sent astronauts to the Moon – is one of the greatest achievements in human history.

A new, much larger rocket was required to launch the large and complex command and landing modules into space and to the Moon. This rocket is still the largest, heaviest and most powerful ever launched.

After a series of test launches, including one mission to the moon which did not land (Apollo 10), Apollo 11, carrying astronauts Neil Armstrong, Buzz Aldrin and Michael Collins, launched from Cape Canaveral in July 1969. After the launch, their command/service module (CSM) extracted and docked with the Lunar module (LM), which was stored in the rocket section below. With both modules in their docked configuration (right) they travelled to the Moon and entered lunar orbit. Armstrong and Aldrin then descended to the Moon's surface in the lunar module. Neil Armstrong was the first of the pair to step onto the Moon, uttering the famous words, "One small step for man, one giant leap for mankind". Aldrin joined him, and together they took photographs, and collected samples of moon rock and dust.

They then re-entered the lander, launched the ascent stage and returned to join Michael Collins in the CSM for their return to Earth.

Five more successful Apollo missions followed. The final three missions included the transportation of a moon vehicle along with the Lunar lander. This electrically-powered lunar rover vehicle (LRV – right) allowed the astronauts to travel further on the Moon's surface, travelling nearly 8km away from their landing site.

The final Apollo mission, Apollo 17, returned to Earth in December 1972. It was the last time an astronaut stood on the surface of the Moon.

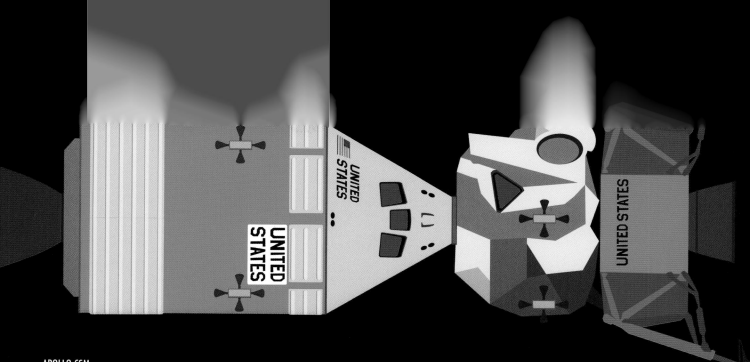

APOLLO CSM
Length: 11 m
Diameter: 3.9 m
Weight: 14,690 kg

APOLLO LM
Length: 7 m
Diameter: 9.4 m
Weight: 15,200 kg

APOLLO LRV
Length: 3.1 m
Width: 2. 3 m
Height: 1.1 m
Weight: 210 kg

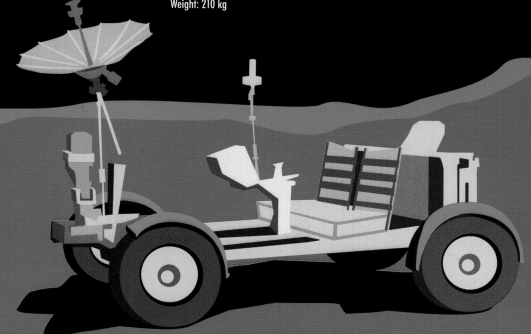

THE SPACE SHUTTLE

NASA's Space Transportation System (STS), more commonly known as the Space Shuttle, was an American spacecraft that launched 135 times during its 30 years of service between 1981 and 2011.

The Orbiter Vehicle (OV) was the spaceplane component of the Space Shuttle. It had a large payload bay (to carry cargo) enabling it to deliver satellites into Earth's orbit, perform maintenance and add new parts to space telescopes like Hubble and Chandra. In addition, this allowed it to perform a major role in the construction of the International Space Station (ISS). It could also carry a laboratory in its bay, which was known as Spacelab. This was used to perform science experiments in space before the ISS was operational.

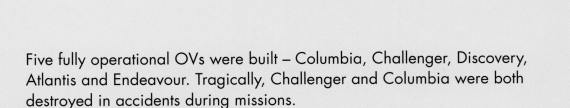

Five fully operational OVs were built – Columbia, Challenger, Discovery, Atlantis and Endeavour. Tragically, Challenger and Columbia were both destroyed in accidents during missions.

The complete launch vehicle (pictured on p.67) was made up of a reusable OV, two reusable solid fuel booster rockets, and an expendable external fuel tank. The STS launch vehicle was capable of delivering the OV to a typical mission altitude of 320 km. The maximum altitude the Space Shuttle operated at was 618 km, during repairs to the Hubble Space Telescope.

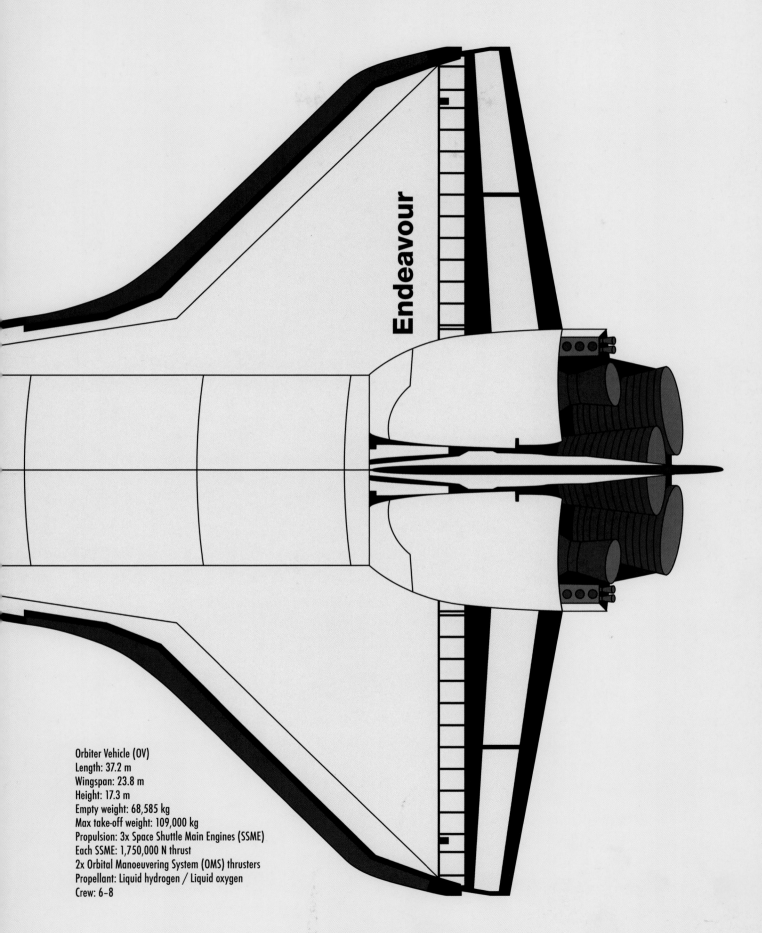

Endeavour

Orbiter Vehicle (OV)
Length: 37.2 m
Wingspan: 23.8 m
Height: 17.3 m
Empty weight: 68,585 kg
Max take-off weight: 109,000 kg
Propulsion: 3x Space Shuttle Main Engines (SSME)
Each SSME: 1,750,000 N thrust
2x Orbital Manoeuvering System (OMS) thrusters
Propellant: Liquid hydrogen / Liquid oxygen
Crew: 6–8

ARTIFICIAL SATELLITES

Since the launch of Sputnik, artificial satellites have become one of the most important aspects of space exploration and the space industry. Initially used to test engineering principles and for scientific research they have since been used for a wide range of important tasks. Such roles include communications, navigation, weather detection, spying, television transmission, and internet connectivity.

Satellites are usually delivered to Earth orbit by unmanned launch vehicles. The simplest and cheapest orbit to place a satellite is low Earth orbit, which we will learn about on p.60. There are also other Earth orbits that are more suited to specific purposes.

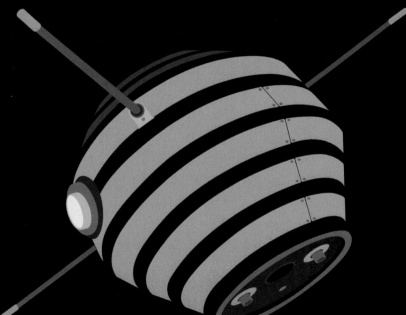

ASTERIX
Country: France
Launched: 26 November 1965
Length: 0.55 m
Diameter: 0.53 m
Weight: 42 kg
Altitude: 527–1,697 km

Asterix was the first French satellite in space. Launched from the Hammaguir launch site in western Algeria, it was the first satellite that wasn't launched on either an American or Soviet launch vehicle. The mission was designed to test both the Diamant rocket and the satellite technology itself. Unfortunately, because of damage to its antennae, contact was lost with Asterix shortly after it reached orbit. However, it is still in Earth orbit!

EXPLORER 1
Country: USA
Launched: 31 January 1958
Length: 2 m
Diameter: 0.15 m
Weight: 14 kg
Altitude: 358–2,550 km

Explorer 1 was the first satellite launched by the USA, and the third satellite in space after the USSR's Sputnik 1 and 2. It carried a radiation detector, thermometers and a device to detect impacts from micrometeorites. It had a transmitter to broadcast data back to Earth. Contact was lost with Explorer during May the same year, but it remained in orbit for 12 more years.

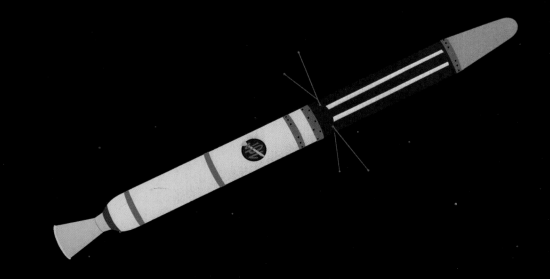

OSUMI

Country: Japan
Launched: 11 February 1970
Length: 1 m
Diameter: 0.48 m
Weight: 24 kg
Altitude: 350–5,140 km

Osumi was Japan's first satellite in space. It carried basic equipment to measure acceleration and temperature, with transmitters to relay this information back to Earth. Its broadcast signal became weaker over the 24 hours after launch, until it was lost. The satellite remained in space until 2003, when it burned up during re-entry over North Africa.

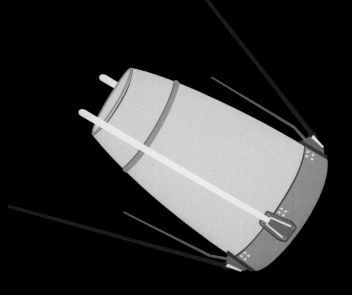

TELSTAR 1

Country: USA
Launched: 10 July 1962
Length: 0.87 m
Diameter: 0.87 m
Weight: 171 kg
Altitude: 952–5,933 km

Telstar was an experimental communications satellite. It paved the way for many of the telecommunications technologies that we enjoy today, such as satellite television and international telephone connections. It carried a transponder – a device that allowed it to relay signals from one position on Earth and 'bounce' them to another location. This allowed the first live television broadcast between the USA and Europe, and the first satellite telephone call. It went out of service in 1963, but is still in Earth orbit.

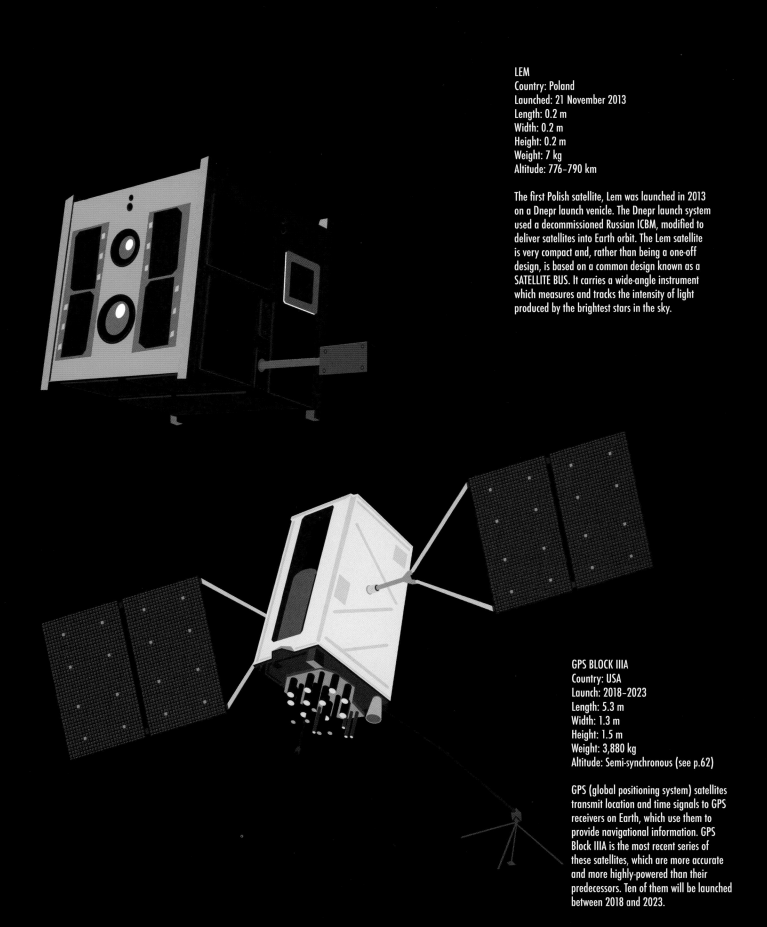

LEM
Country: Poland
Launched: 21 November 2013
Length: 0.2 m
Width: 0.2 m
Height: 0.2 m
Weight: 7 kg
Altitude: 776–790 km

The first Polish satellite, Lem was launched in 2013 on a Dnepr launch venicle. The Dnepr launch system used a decommissioned Russian ICBM, modified to deliver satellites into Earth orbit. The Lem satellite is very compact and, rather than being a one-off design, is based on a common design known as a SATELLITE BUS. It carries a wide-angle instrument which measures and tracks the intensity of light produced by the brightest stars in the sky.

GPS BLOCK IIIA
Country: USA
Launch: 2018–2023
Length: 5.3 m
Width: 1.3 m
Height: 1.5 m
Weight: 3,880 kg
Altitude: Semi-synchronous (see p.62)

GPS (global positioning system) satellites transmit location and time signals to GPS receivers on Earth, which use them to provide navigational information. GPS Block IIIA is the most recent series of these satellites, which are more accurate and more highly-powered than their predecessors. Ten of them will be launched between 2018 and 2023.

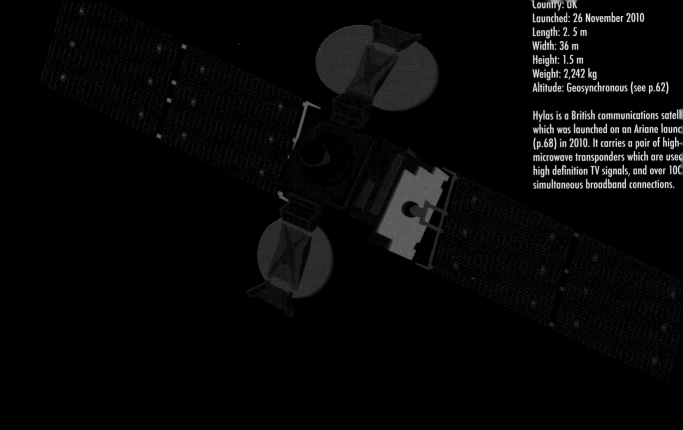

Country: UK
Launched: 26 November 2010
Length: 2. 5 m
Width: 36 m
Height: 1.5 m
Weight: 2,242 kg
Altitude: Geosynchronous (see p.62)

Hylas is a British communications satell
which was launched on an Ariane launc
(p.68) in 2010. It carries a pair of high-
microwave transponders which are used
high definition TV signals, and over 10C
simultaneous broadband connections.

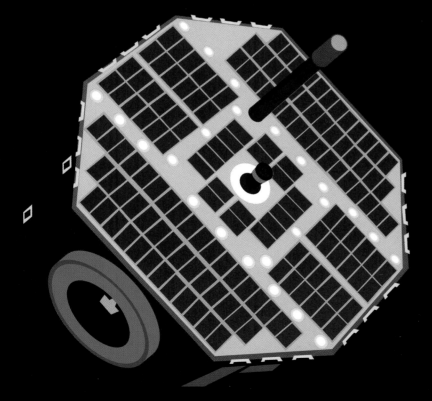

IBEX
Country: USA
Launched: 19 October 2008
Length: 0.58 m
Diameter: 0.95 m
Weight: 107 kg
Altitude: 59,190–312,199 km

Ibex, or the Interstellar Boundary Explore
is a NASA satellite which launched in
2008. Its mission is to study the edge of
the Solar System, and the way in which
particles from the Sun interact with the
particles that make up interstellar space.
It follows a highly elliptical orbit so it car
perform its imaging tasks well away from
the effects of the Earth's magnetic field.

EARTH ORBITS

he easiest and least expensive orbit to place a satellite or a spacecraft is low Earth orbit,
r LEO. This is the area of space surrounding the Earth, above the atmosphere, to an
ltitude of 2000 km. Apart from the Apollo missions to the Moon, all human spaceflight
as taken place in LEO. Most satellites are in LEO, especially imaging and weather
atellites which benefit from the increased detail available at lower altitudes.

298–1374 km
Gemini 11

215–939 km
Sputnik

781km
Iridium satellite

538 km
Hubble Space Telescope

408km
ISS

160 km
Lower edge of LEO

The diagram below compares the positions of various satellites and spacecraft in LEO. As you can see, the International Space Station (ISS) maintains a relatively low altitude position. This is mainly because of the expense of delivering cargo and spare parts to the ISS.

All satellites in LEO experience a degree of drag, as there is a very small but still noticeable amount of atmospheric gas at LEO altitudes. As a result, satellites need to perform occasional engine burns in order to speed up to return to their correct altitudes. Otherwise their orbits will gradually decay until they burn up during re-entry.

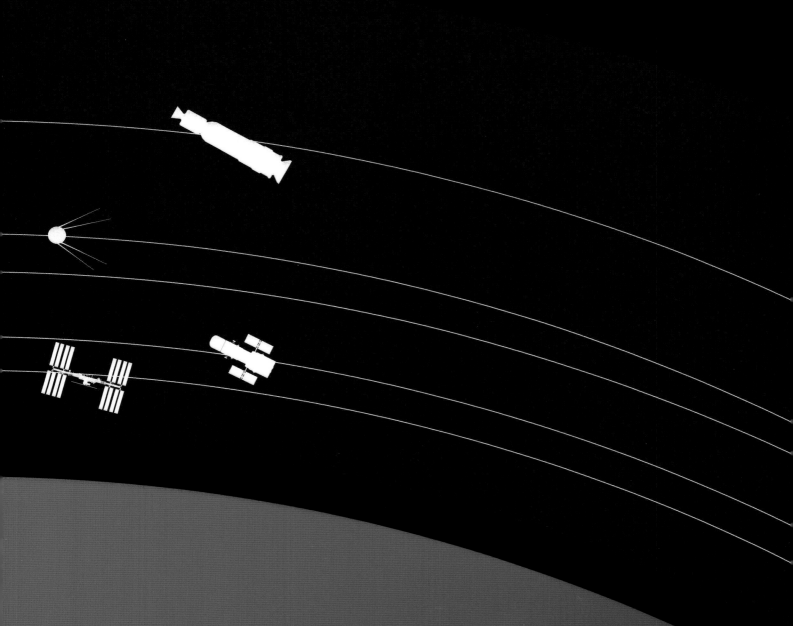

OTHER EARTH ORBITS

It is more expensive to deliver satellites to higher altitude orbits, but there are a number of reasons to do so. One of the most important orbits is called GEOSYNCHRONOUS. This is an orbit on which the orbital speed matches the rotation of the Earth, so the satellite returns to the same point in the sky every 24 hours. A semi-synchronous orbit is similar, but the orbital period is 12 hours, so it returns to the same point twice a day. Most navigational satellites (such as GPS) are on semi-synchronous orbits. The area between LEO and geosyncronous orbit is called medium Earth orbit or MEO.

Some satellites orbiting in MEO are described in the diagram below.

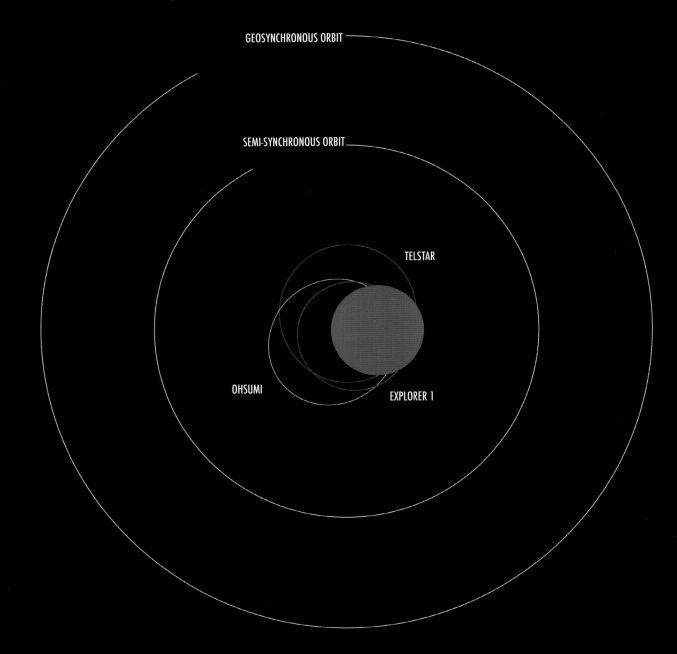

The Interstellar Boundary Explorer – IBEX – described on p.59 orbits in an elliptical high Earth orbit (HEO), which passes through much higher altitudes than a geosynchronous orbit. As you can see in the diagram below, the orbit of IBEX passes relatively close to the orbit of the Moon.

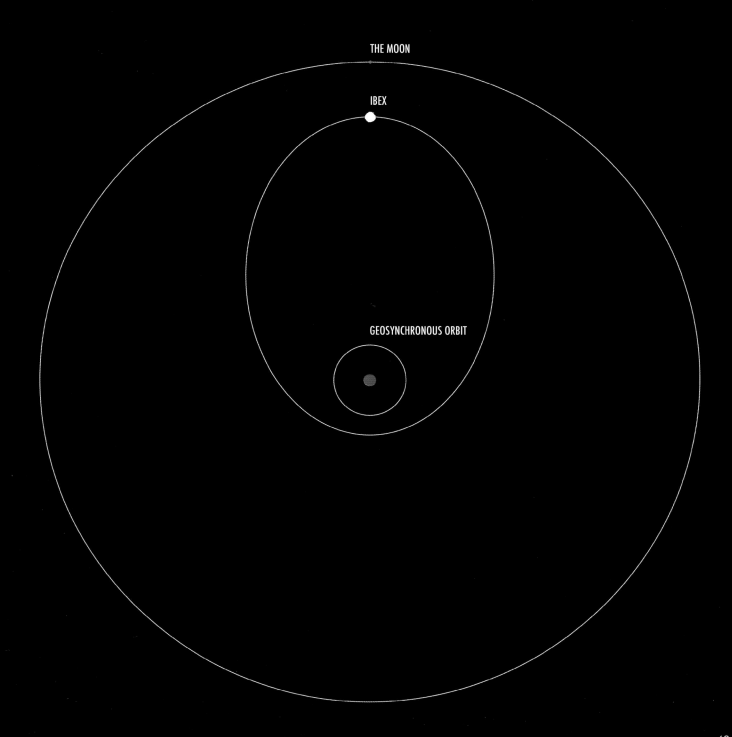

THE MOON

IBEX

GEOSYNCHRONOUS ORBIT

LAUNCH VEHICLES

Launching spacecraft into Earth orbit and beyond is very difficult. Every spacecraft, from a tiny satellite to a large manned craft such as the Space Shuttle, requires a powerful rocket system to fire it into space. Such systems are called LAUNCH VEHICLES. Because of the strong pull of gravity, a launch vehicle needs to increase its speed to a certain level before its fuel runs out.

For a spacecraft to enter a stable low Earth orbit it needs to achieve an orbital velocity of 7.8 km/s, or 28,080 km/h. This is very fast! To produce sufficient acceleration, such a spacecraft needs to carry a lot of fuel. In fact, the mass of most large launch vehicles is at least 90% fuel.

To further reduce the effects of gravity, larger launch vehicles are constructed with separate, stacked stages. The stages fire in order and, as each stage runs out of fuel, it is jettisoned to reduce the overall weight of the remaining spacecraft.

Thanks to advances in materials and engine technology, launch vehicles have become more efficient. They can lift larger loads using less fuel, and so delivering cargo into space is less expensive. There are also new developments, such as rocket stages that return to the launch site rather than falling into the ocean and being lost.

For many years the colossal Apollo-era Saturn V rockets have remained the largest, most powerful launch vehicles ever built, However, a new generation of heavy lift rockets are currently being developed. These will surpass the lifting capacity of Saturn V, and open up new possibilities in space exploration!

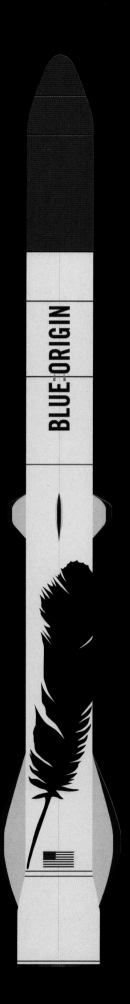

BLUE ORIGIN NEW GLENN
Country: USA
In service: Proposed launch 2020
Length: 95 m
Diameter: 7 m
Weight: TBC

New Glenn is a powerful new launch vehicle currently being developed by the private American space company Blue Origin. Designed to work as a two or three-stage rocket, it features a reusable first stage that will be able to return to Earth to be reused up to 100 times. The first New Glenn launches are due to be deliveries of satellites into geosynchronous orbit.

EARLY LAUNCH VEHICLES

The first space launch vehicles were developed from military missiles, such as the German V2 and the American Redstone. These were not small, but the desire to launch larger and larger spacecraft into orbit required launch vehicles that were substantially bigger. All the launch vehicles over the following pages are to scale.

V2
Country: Germany
In service: 1944–52
Length: 14 m
Diameter: 1.65 m
Weight: 12,500 kg

LITTLE JOE
Country: USA
In service: 1959–60
Length: 15 m
Diameter: 2 m
Weight: 12,700 kg

MERCURY-REDSTONE
Country: USA
In service: 1960–61
Length: 25.4 m
Diameter: 1.7 m
Weight: 30,000 kg

MERCURY-ATLAS
Country: USA
In service: 1960–63
Length: 28.7 m
Diameter: 3 m
Weight: 120,000 kg

R7 SEMYORKA
Country: USSR
In service: 1957
Length: 30 m
Diameter: 3 m
Weight: 267,000 kg

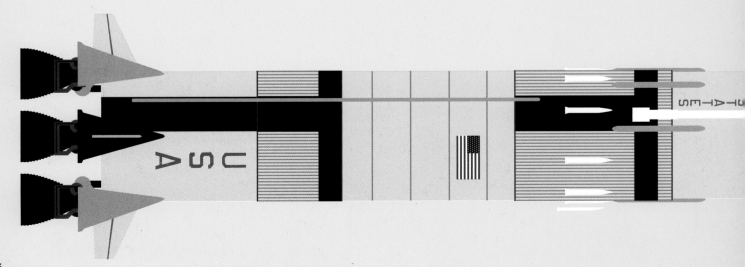

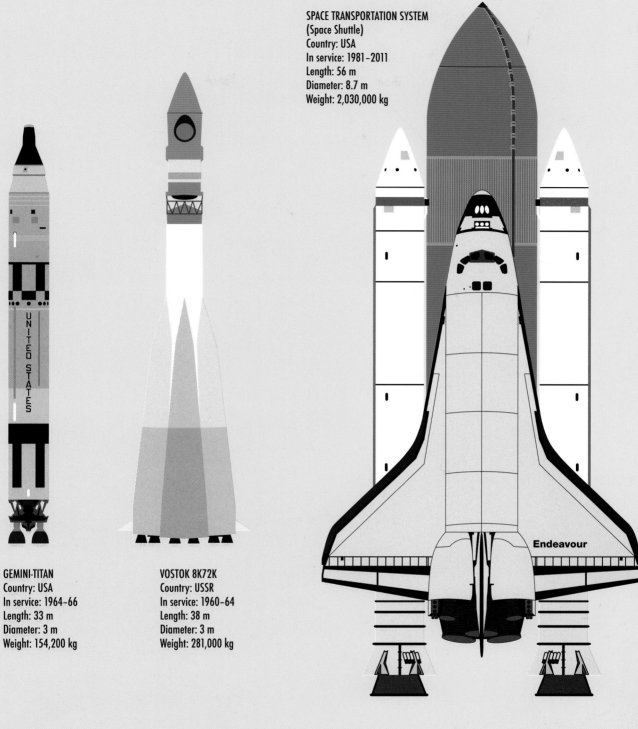

SPACE TRANSPORTATION SYSTEM
(Space Shuttle)
Country: USA
In service: 1981–2011
Length: 56 m
Diameter: 8.7 m
Weight: 2,030,000 kg

Endeavour

GEMINI-TITAN
Country: USA
In service: 1964–66
Length: 33 m
Diameter: 3 m
Weight: 154,200 kg

VOSTOK 8K72K
Country: USSR
In service: 1960–64
Length: 38 m
Diameter: 3 m
Weight: 281,000 kg

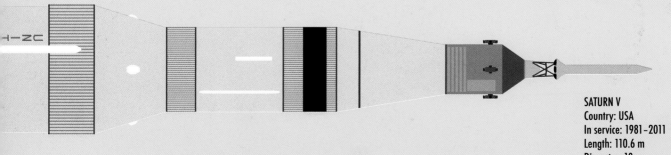

SATURN V
Country: USA
In service: 1981–2011
Length: 110.6 m
Diameter: 10 m
Weight: 2,970,000 kg

LATER LAUNCH VEHICLES

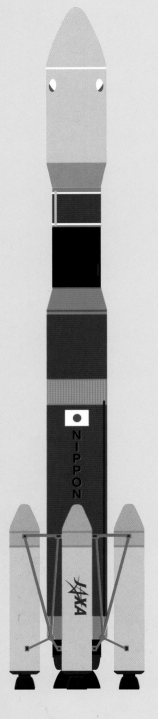

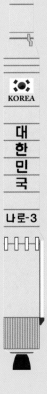

HII-B
Country: Japan
In service: 2009–present
Length: 56.6 m
Diameter: 5.2 m
Weight: 531,000 kg

PSLV
Country: India
In service: 1993–present
Length: 44 m
Diameter: 2.8 m
Weight: 295,000 kg

NARO-1
Country: South Korea
In service: 2009–present
Length: 33 m
Diameter: 3 m
Weight: 140,000 kg

ARIANE-5
Country: Europe
In service: 1996–present
Length: 52 m
Diameter: 5.4 m
Weight: 777,000 kg

In the early days of space travel, America and the Soviet Union were the only countries with the ability to launch space vehicles. Since then, many countries around the world have developed their own spacecraft. Some of these are illustrated here.

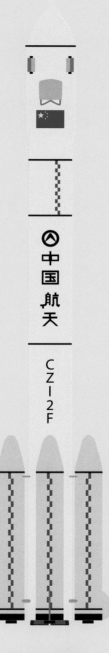

SOYUZ-FG
Country: Russia
In service: 2001–present
Length: 49.5 m
Diameter: 2.95 m
Weight: 305,000 kg

LONG MARCH 2F
Country: China
In service: 1999–present
Length: 62 m
Diameter: 3.4 m
Weight: 464,000 kg

FALCON 9 FT
Country: USA
In service: 2015–present
Length: 71 m
Diameter: 3.6 m
Weight: 549,054 kg

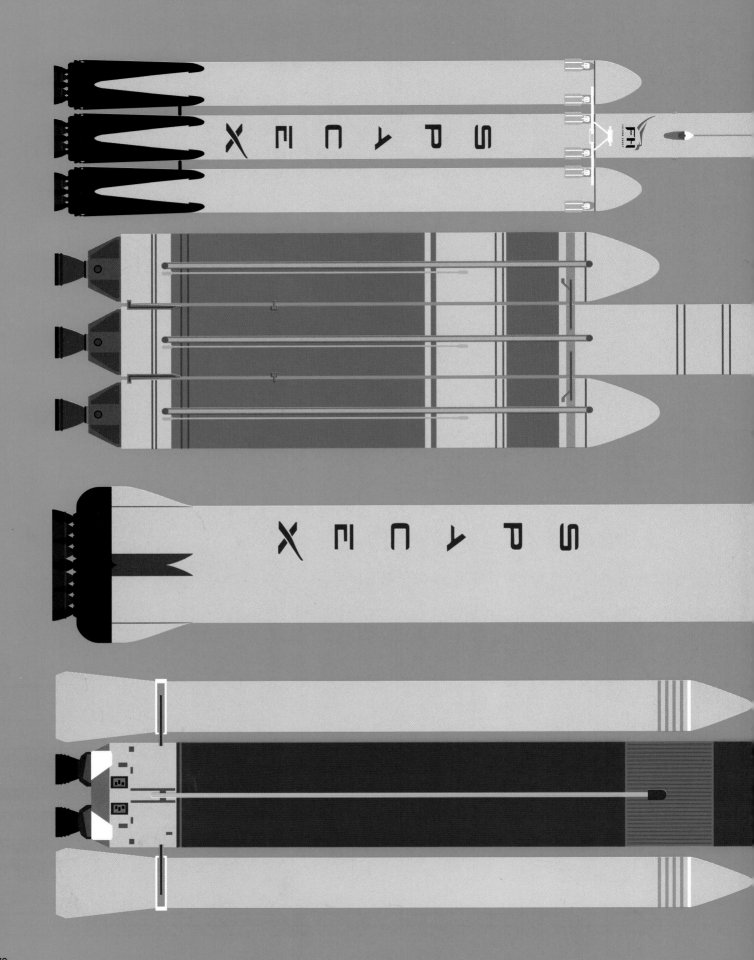

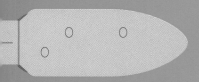

SPACE X FALCON HEAVY
Length: 70 m
Core diameter: 3.6 m
Overall width: 12.2 m
Weight: 1,420,788 kg

HEAVY LIFT VEHICLES

The newest generation of high-power, heavy-lift launch vehicles are being developed for the next steps in human space exploration. Programmes such as the construction of the lunar platform gateway, and missions to the Moon and Mars will require advanced new rocket systems capable of delivering large loads to diverse locations, and often operating unmanned.

DELTA IV HEAVY
Length: 72 m
Core diameter: 5 m
Overall width: 15 m
Weight: 733,000 kg

SPACEX BFR (Proposed)
Length: 106 m
Diameter: 9 m
Weight: 4,400,000 kg

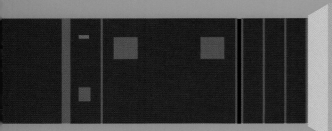

SLS BLOCK 2 CARGO
Length: 111 m
Core diameter: 8.4 m
Overall width: 20 m
Weight: 4,400,000 kg

SCIENCE IN SPACE

One of the central aims of space exploration has been to discover more about the nature of the universe and the scientific explanations for the behaviour of distant stars, planets, galaxies and other astronomical phenomena. In order to gain new understanding about such subjects, many missions, both manned and unmanned, have been sent out into space to discover more about our universe.

Unmanned space probes such as Voyager and Cassini have sent back images from across the Solar System. We have constructed space stations, such as Salyut, Mir, Skylab and the ISS, which have provided us with scientific laboratories in space itself. And space telescopes such as Hubble are able to probe deeply into the distant reaches of the universe, providing imagery of the most ancient galaxies ever discovered.

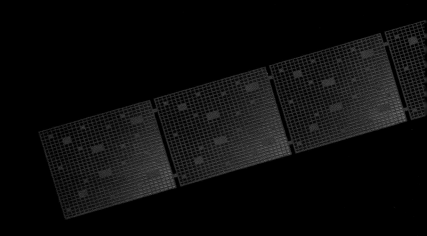

ROSETTA
Length: 2.8 m
Width: 2.1 m
Height: 2 m
Solar array diameter: 32 m
Weight: 2,900 kg

A space probe launched by the European Space
Agency (ESA) in March 2004, Rosetta is perhaps best
known for delivering the Philae module that landed
on the comet 67P/Churyumov-Gerasimenko in
November 2014.

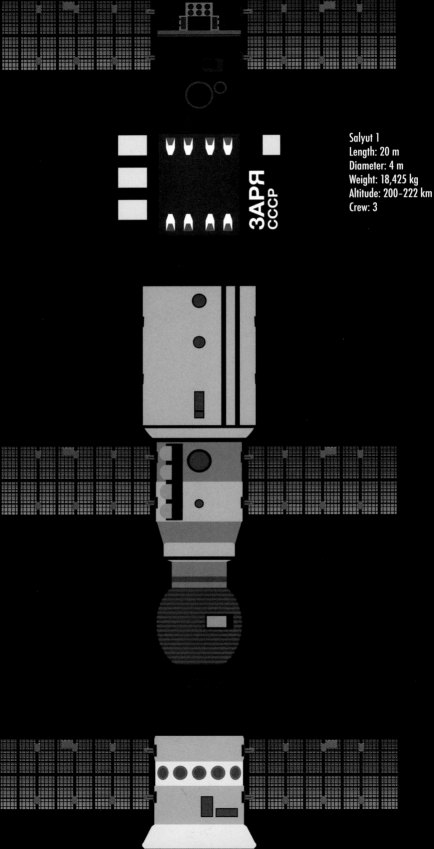

Salyut 1
Length: 20 m
Diameter: 4 m
Weight: 18,425 kg
Altitude: 200–222 km
Crew: 3

ЗАРЯ
CCCP

SALYUT – THE FIRST SPACE STATION

Following the success of the American Apollo programme, the Soviet Union decided to concentrate on the development of manned space stations, rather than attempting their own expeditions to the Moon.

They knew that the USA was planning a space station called Skylab, and this time they wanted to beat the Americans to it.

The first Soviet space station, Salyut 1 (meaning salute), was built in 1970, and was launched by a powerful Proton rocket on 19 April 1971.

The Salyut programme went on to include six more space stations, which featured on board science laboratories and astronomical observatories. Salyut cosmonauts conducted astronomical studies of the Sun, investigated weather patterns on Earth, and the first biological experiments in space.

The final Salyut station, Salyut 7, suffered technical problems and was thought to be lost. A repair mission was launched and cosmonauts managed to reactivate the station's power supply. Because the power problem had crippled the on-board heating system, the cosmonauts were dressed in specially-made fur-lined spacesuits to protect them from the low temperatures inside the station.

In 1986, the final mission to Salyut 7 transferred equipment to the new modular Mir space station. Salyut 7 was then abandoned, and it deorbited in 1991, breaking up in the skies over northern Argentina.

SKYLAB

Skylab was the first space station constructed by the American space agency NASA. Launched in May 1973 using an unmanned modified Saturn V rocket, it suffered considerable damage during delivery into Earth orbit. Its shielding was destroyed, and its solar arrays were unable to extend properly, meaning the station had a very restricted power supply.

The first manned mission to Skylab launched later that month, and the astronauts undertook repair work to make the station habitable. Two more missions followed. The longest of these – Skylab-4 – lasted 84 days which, at the time, was a record for the longest human stay in space.

Many scientific experiments took place on Skylab, including imaging of the surface of the Sun, which proved the existence of holes in the Sun's corona layer.

The members of the Skylab-4 mission returned to Earth in February 1974. Skylab itself re-entered Earth's atmosphere in July 1979, breaking up and scattering its debris in Western Australia.

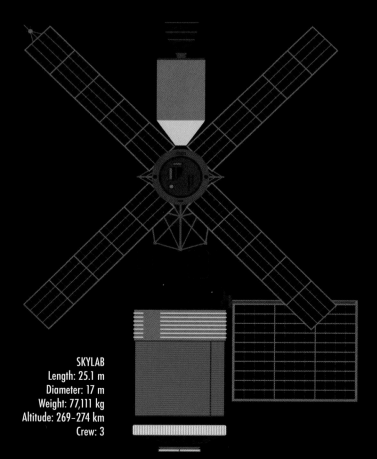

SKYLAB
Length: 25.1 m
Diameter: 17 m
Weight: 77,111 kg
Altitude: 269–274 km
Crew: 3

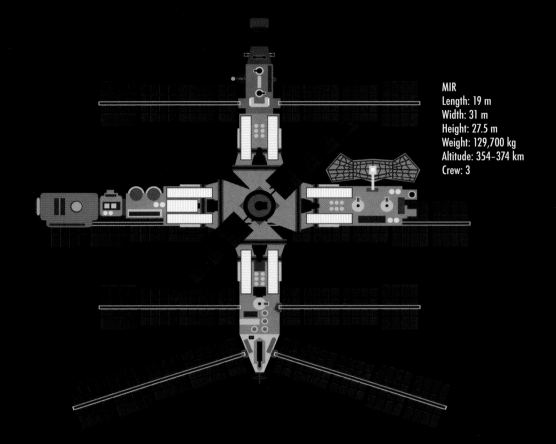

MIR
Length: 19 m
Width: 31 m
Height: 27.5 m
Weight: 129,700 kg
Altitude: 354–374 km
Crew: 3

MIR

Mir was the second Soviet space station project, following Salyut. Unlike Salyut and Skylab, Mir was modular, constructed from separate components which were delivered to low Earth orbit between 1986 and 1996. It was primarily designed as a laboratory and testing environment for space medicine and space science in general.

The Space Shuttle Atlantis docked with Mir in 1995, and returned in 1996 on another mission which featured the first joint USA-Russia spacewalk.

The Russian cosmonaut Valeri Polyakov still holds the record for the longest single stay in space – he spent 437 days in space during a mission on Mir between 1994 and 1995.

Mir was designed to last five years, but ended up in service for fifteen. Eventually, with the launch of the ISS project, the decision was made to take Mir out of service. It was deorbited in March 2001, and its debris fell in the South Pacific near Fiji.

INTERNATIONAL SPACE STATION

The largest man-made object in space, the International Space Station is a collaboration between five space agencies – NASA (USA), ESA (Europe), Roscosmos (Russia), JAXA (Japan) and CSA (Canada). It is a large, modular satellite in low Earth orbit.

The first crew mission launched in November 2000 on a Russian Soyuz spacecraft. Since then the ISS has been continuously occupied, with a full crew of six astronauts or cosmonauts at any one time.

Most early missions to the ISS were focused on construction, using robotic arms to move the various components into place. Maintenance remains a major part of life on the ISS. Many parts require repair or replacement over time. This means astronauts on board always have lots to do!

Astronauts on the ISS spend much of their time performing scientific experiments. This includes investigations into the effects of space on the human body. Other experiments investigate the nature of space itself, including the capture of space dust, which is analysed in the search for evidence of life from other planets.

Mealtimes are complicated affairs, with food carefully packaged inside sealed bags and tubes. Fresh food arrives on resupply craft from Earth, but the rest of the time it is food that has been processed so it can be stored for long periods. Any liquids, such as drinks or soups, are consumed from a pouch using a straw.

Astronauts wash in a special cubicle, using a water spray and wet wipes. Toilets use powerful suction to remove waste. The astronauts' urine is processed and reused as drinking water.

When it is time for bed astronauts crawl inside sleeping bags, which are tethered to the walls of special sleeping booths.

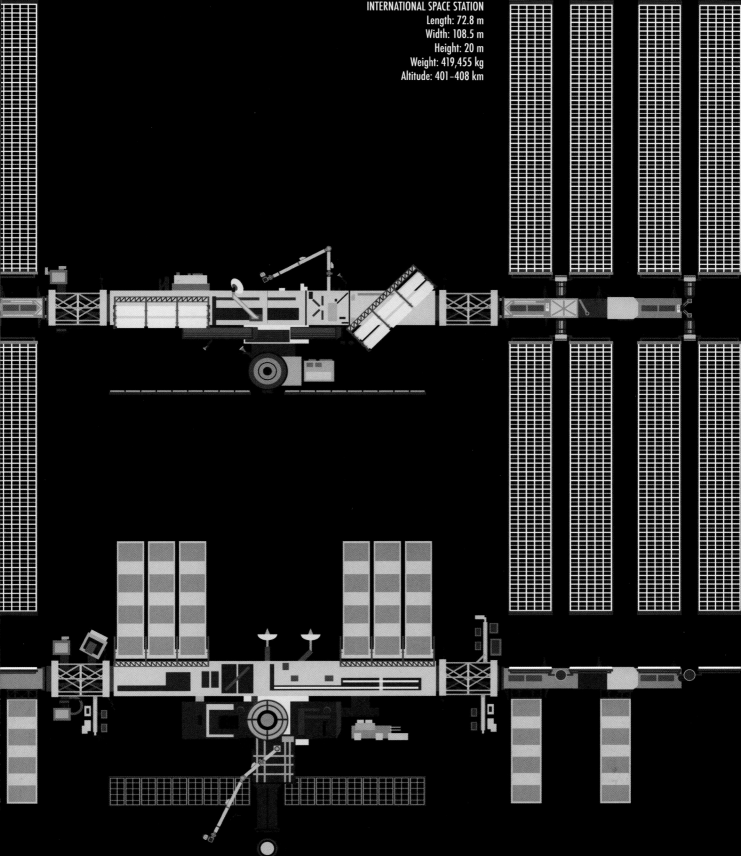

INTERNATIONAL SPACE STATION
Length: 72.8 m
Width: 108.5 m
Height: 20 m
Weight: 419,455 kg
Altitude: 401–408 km

SPACE PROBES

In the sixty years since Sputnik was launched, much of the Solar System has been explored by unmanned spacecraft. These interplanetary vehicles, known as space probes, have sometimes travelled remarkable distances from Earth. Although they are often compact, compared with spacecraft designed to carry humans, they nevertheless require hugely complicated feats of technological development in order to perform their mission aims. For example, because of the length of many of these missions, probes need long-term power sources to keep them running for many years. Some are able to generate this energy using solar arrays, while others have used atomic power generators.

Moving towards the furthest reaches of the Solar System requires a series of engine burns. Many probes are propelled by conventionally-fuelled rocket engines, but others have pioneered novel propulsion systems, such as electrical ion thrusters.

JUNO
Length: 4.6 m
Diameter: 20.1 m
Weight: 3,625 kg

Juno is a NASA space probe, currently in orbit around the planet Jupiter. It carries on board a selection of scientific instruments which are being used to study Jupiter's atmosphere, magnetic and gravitational fields, and rotational movement. The aim of the mission is to shed light on how Jupiter was formed, and what is responsible for its extreme atmospheric conditions. At the end of its mission Juno will be sent into Jupiter's atmosphere where it will burn up.

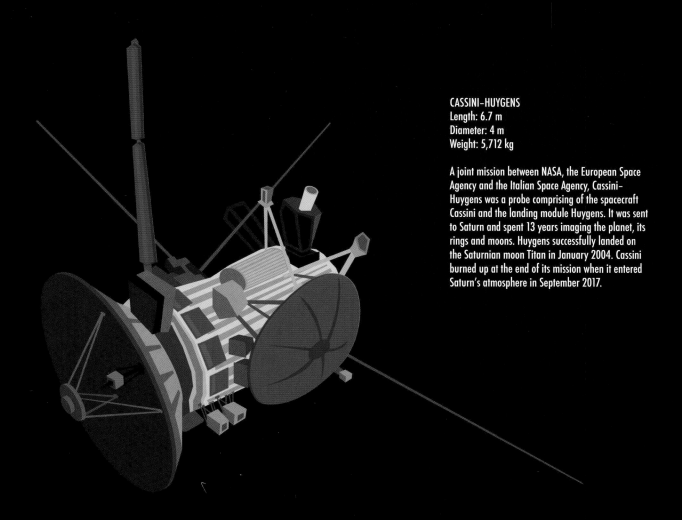

CASSINI-HUYGENS
Length: 6.7 m
Diameter: 4 m
Weight: 5,712 kg

A joint mission between NASA, the European Space Agency and the Italian Space Agency, Cassini-Huygens was a probe comprising of the spacecraft Cassini and the landing module Huygens. It was sent to Saturn and spent 13 years imaging the planet, its rings and moons. Huygens successfully landed on the Saturnian moon Titan in January 2004. Cassini burned up at the end of its mission when it entered Saturn's atmosphere in September 2017.

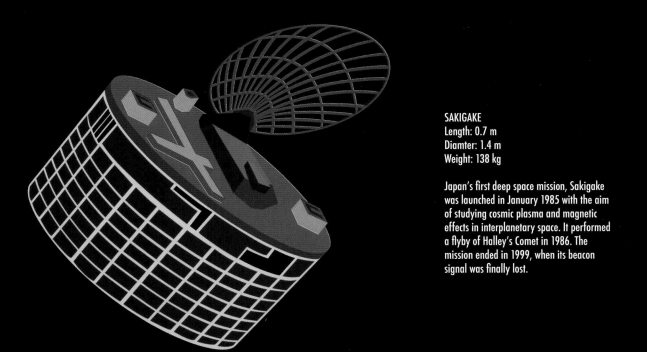

SAKIGAKE
Length: 0.7 m
Diamter: 1.4 m
Weight: 138 kg

Japan's first deep space mission, Sakigake was launched in January 1985 with the aim of studying cosmic plasma and magnetic effects in interplanetary space. It performed a flyby of Halley's Comet in 1986. The mission ended in 1999, when its beacon signal was finally lost.

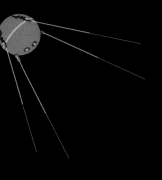

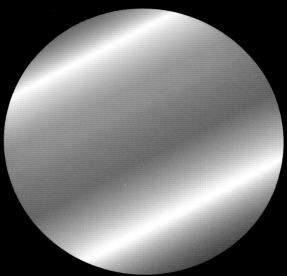

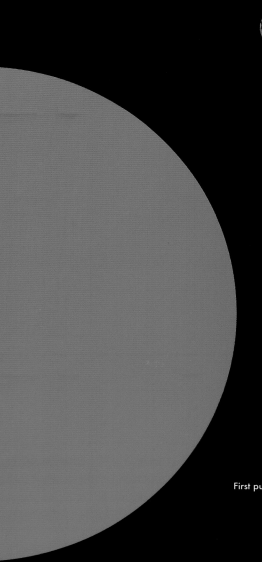

First published in the United Kingdom in 2018 by
Pavilion Children's Books
43 Great Ormond Street
London
WC1N 3HZ

An imprint of Pavilion Books Limited.

Publisher and Editor: Neil Dunnicliffe
Assistant Editor: Hattie Grylls
Art Director: Anna Lubecka

ISBN: 9781843653745

A CIP catalogue record for this book is available from the British Library.

10 9 8 7 6 5 4 3 2 1

Reproduction by Rival Colour UK

Printed by Leefung Printing Ltd, China

This book can be ordered directly from the publisher online
at www.pavilionbooks.com, or try your local bookshop.

CONTENTS

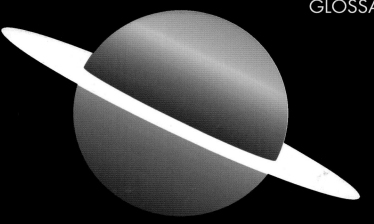

SPACE TELESCOPES

Because of interference from atmospheric pollution, telescope observatories on Earth are limited in how far they can see and how well. Telescopes launched into space, although very expensive, are able to 'look' much further and with more detail.

The Hubble Space Telescope (below) was launched on board the Space Shuttle in April 1990. It is designed to image space phenomena using mostly visible light (rather than x-rays or radio waves) and it has produced highly-detailed photographs of space objects including some of the most distant galaxies, the magnificent Carina nebula, aurorae and supernovae. It has also played an important role in understanding black holes and the origins of the universe.

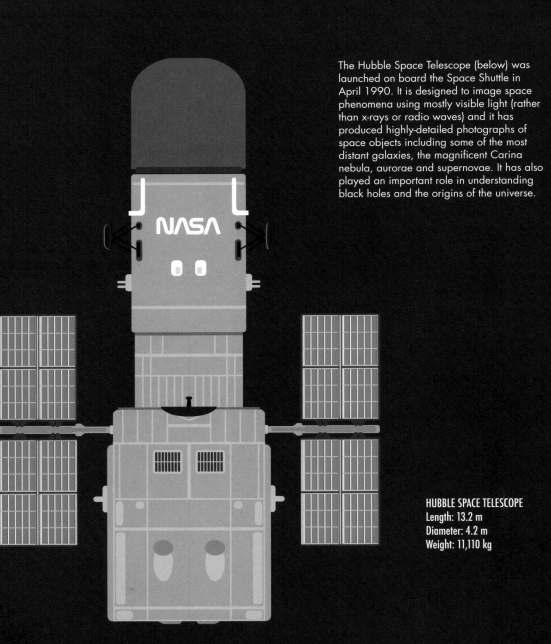

HUBBLE SPACE TELESCOPE
Length: 13.2 m
Diameter: 4.2 m
Weight: 11,110 kg

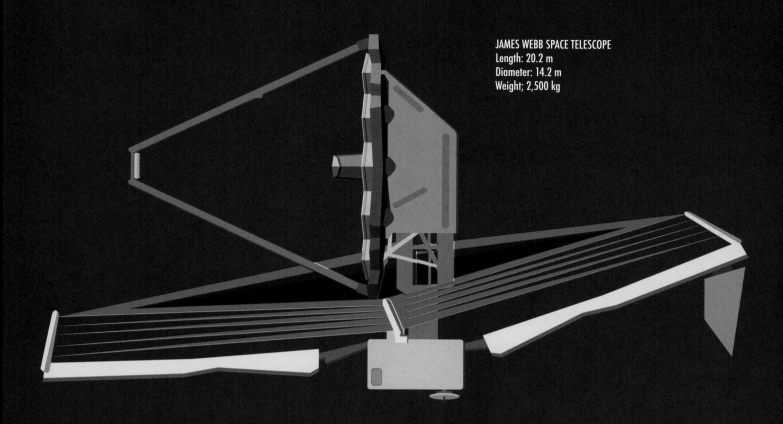

JAMES WEBB SPACE TELESCOPE
Length: 20.2 m
Diameter: 14.2 m
Weight; 2,500 kg

The successor to Hubble is the James Webb Space Telescope (above). This is due to launch in 2019, and carries an even bigger optical mirror than the one used by Hubble. The mirror sizes are compared in the diagram (below). The JWST will record images mainly in the infrared light spectrum, and its great resolving power will allow it to take images of star formation in molecular clouds, galaxy cores, and distant exoplanets.

Hubble Telescope Mirror
Diameter: 2.4 m
Material: aluminium reflective surface on glass base, with magnesium flouride protective layer

Webb Telescope Mirror Array
Diameter: 6.5 m
Material: gold-coated beryllium

ASTRONOMY

What is astronomy? It is the name we use to describe the science of space.

Observation of the night sky is a fundamental aspect of astronomy. Originally this was done with the naked eye. In the 17th century the telescope was invented, which allowed astronomers to see much further into space, and observe the planets in more detail. Since then, scientists have built bigger and bigger telescopes, including ones which can 'see' things that our eyes can't, like x-rays, infrared and even radio waves. We have even launched telescopes into space!

Astronomers use maths to calculate and describe the movement of planets, stars and other bodies through space. The same techniques can be used by ASTRONAUTS to navigate their spacecraft. If you want to become an astronaut one day, you need to work hard in maths lessons!

Astronomers use the theories of physics to understand the mechanics and structure of the universe. The astronomical discoveries of the Renaissance provided laws which offer very accurate descriptions of how bodies (e.g. planets) in space interact with each other. Since then, advances in physics have allowed us to explain other phenomena. We now know how stars such as the Sun create both energy and chemical elements in their cores. We have proved the existence of BLACK HOLES and gravitational waves, and confirmed these discoveries by observation.

Astronomers use the science of chemistry to discover what distant bodies are made of. By analysing observations from radio telescopes, they can detect the presence of different chemical elements and molecules in the far reaches of space.

Because of the hard work performed by astronomers and scientists over the centuries, we now possess an amazing degree of knowledge and understanding of the nature and history of the universe.

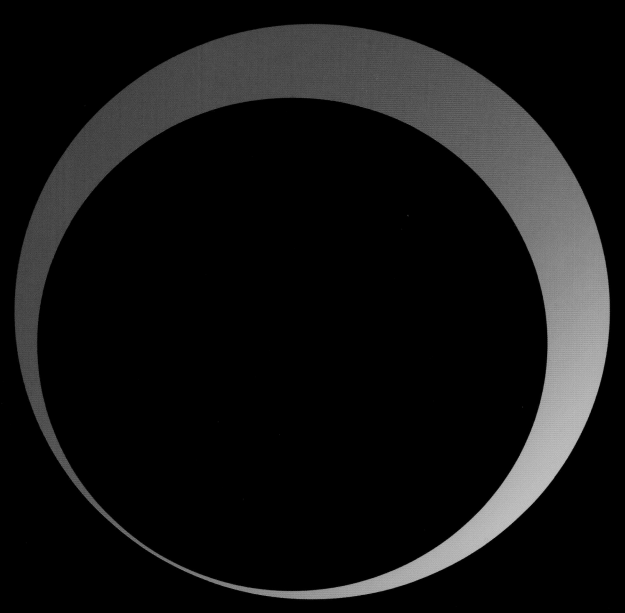

SOLAR ECLIPSE

Eclipses of the Sun are some of the most dramatic astronomical phenomena that can be viewed from Earth.

When the Moon passes between the Earth and the Sun, it casts a shadow which obscures our view of the Sun. Most solar eclipses are partial (large illustration above), when the Sun and Moon are not in line with the Earth, and so the Moon only obscures part of the Sun.

When they are lined up and the Moon obscures the whole of the Sun, it is known as a total eclipse (right). A total eclipse results in a dark sky, and reveals the faint CORONA which surrounds the sun.

SPACE LAUNCH SYSTEM

Since the final mission of the Space Shuttle programme in 2011, America has relied on the Russian space agency Roscosmos to deliver NASA astronauts to the ISS on its Soyuz-TMA spacecraft.

NASA are working hard to develop their new spacecraft, the Space Launch System (SLS). The SLS is based around a multi-stage rocket which, in its final form, will be the most powerful rocket ever built. It will be even more powerful than SpaceX's Falcon Heavy, or NASA's previous Saturn V!

The SLS programme will be capable of delivering cargo beyond low Earth orbit, in the form of the SLS Cargo (pp.70-71). This will be essential in the construction of the Lunar Orbital Platform-Gateway (p.90). The LOP-G components include a heavy power and propulsion section which will need a powerful rocket to deliver it into position.

SLS also has a manned version, the SLS Crew. This will carry a new spacecraft, called Orion. Orion combines a command capsule and a service module. The command capsule can carry up to six astronauts, and features advanced computers and an automatic docking system. The service module carries fuel and a propulsion system for orbital transfer and manoeuvring, along with oxygen and water supplies for the crew. It also features retractable solar arrays which generate power for the entire spacecraft.

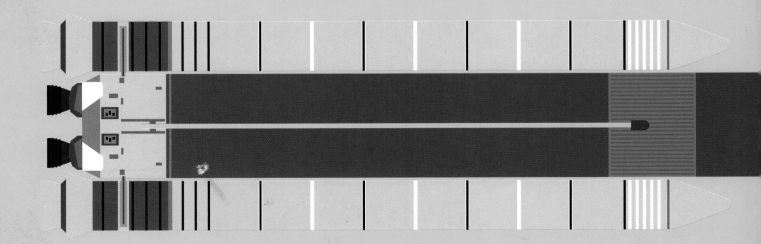

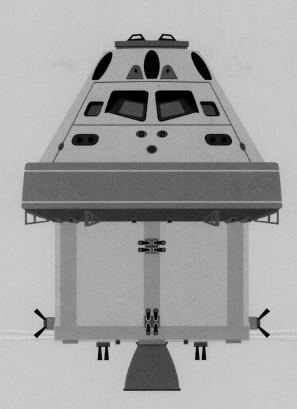

ORION MULTI-PURPOSE CREW VEHICLE (MPCV)
Length: 5 m
Width: 3.3 m
Capsule weight: 10,387 kg
Service module weight: 15,461 kg
Crew: 4–6

Orion performed a successful unmanned test when it was launched by a Delta IV heavy rocket in December 2014. The first manned Orion mission is currently planned for 2022.

SLS BLOCK 1B CREW
Length: 110.9 m
Diameter (core stage): 8.4 m

The 1B Crew is the version of the SLS heavy-lift launch system (details on pp.70-71) that is designed to carry the Orion capsule to the LOP-G. Like the Cargo variant, it uses a combination of two solid fuel booster rockets with a four-engine core stage. This is then followed by the four-engine Exploration Upper Stage.

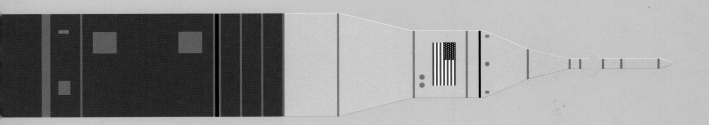

THE BOOK OF FIXED STARS

Abd al-Rahman al-Sufi, also known as Azophi, was an Abbasid astronomer who lived between 903 and 986 CE in Isfahan (in modern day Iran). He was one of the most important Islamic astronomers, and studied Ptolemy's findings carefully.

His own work was called *The Book of Fixed Stars*. It included precise drawings of the constellations, such as Cepheus (below left), Virgo (left) and Ursa Major (below right). He was also the first person to observe and record other galaxies, including the Andromeda Galaxy and the Large Magellanic Cloud.

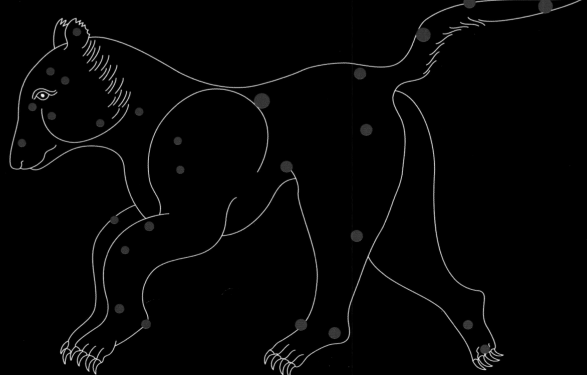

MISSION TO MARS

A manned journey to Mars would be the most complex and brave space mission ever attempted. To reach Mars using the minimum amount of energy, the Deep Space Transport (DST) would perform a manoeuvre from Earth to Mars known as a HOHMANN TRANSFER ORBIT. This requires two engine burns. The first burn (Day 0 below) moves the DST from the orbit of Earth around the Sun, into an elliptical orbit (yellow) – the Hohmann transfer orbit. This orbit meets the Martian orbit after 259 days. A second burn is performed at Day 259, which moves the DST from the transfer orbit to Martian orbit.

Because the Earth and Mars orbit the Sun at different speeds, Mars effectively catches up with the DST during its orbit. As you can see, at Day 0, Mars is quite distant from its eventual position at Day 259.

Once the DST is in orbit around Mars, it can launch its lander module on to the surface of Mars.

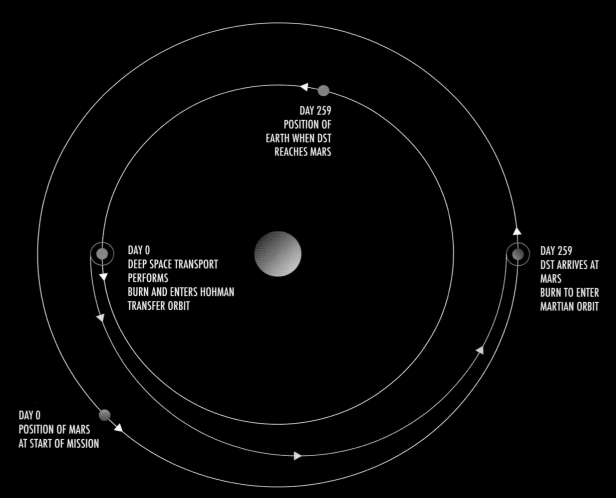

DAY 259
POSITION OF
EARTH WHEN DST
REACHES MARS

DAY 0
DEEP SPACE TRANSPORT
PERFORMS
BURN AND ENTERS HOHMAN
TRANSFER ORBIT

DAY 259
DST ARRIVES AT
MARS
BURN TO ENTER
MARTIAN ORBIT

DAY 0
POSITION OF MARS
AT START OF MISSION

This is achieved by performing a burn that deorbits the lander module. When the Mars landing mission is completed, the ascent stage of the lander launches from the surface of Mars and returns to the orbiting DST. The DST can then return when Earth and Mars are properly aligned, either within 2 weeks, or not until 18 months later. This means the minimum duration of a Mars mission would be 632 days, and the next shortest would be nearly 3 years!

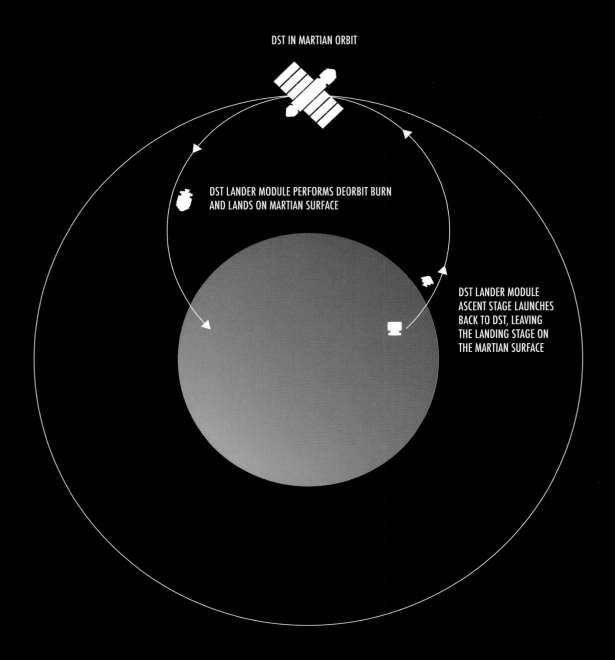

DST IN MARTIAN ORBIT

DST LANDER MODULE PERFORMS DEORBIT BURN
AND LANDS ON MARTIAN SURFACE

DST LANDER MODULE
ASCENT STAGE LAUNCHES
BACK TO DST, LEAVING
THE LANDING STAGE ON
THE MARTIAN SURFACE

PLANETARY MOTION

In the 17th century, the German astronomer Johannes Kepler developed the Copernican system further. He studied the motion of the planets in greater detail and realised that the paths they followed around the Sun were not circular, as had been previously thought.

Between 1609 and 1619 Kepler produced his Laws of Planetary Motion, which remain accurate tools for calculating the orbits of planets around a much bigger object such as the Sun. Although Kepler could only observe the planets as far out as Jupiter and Saturn, his laws work perfectly to describe Uranus and Neptune too.

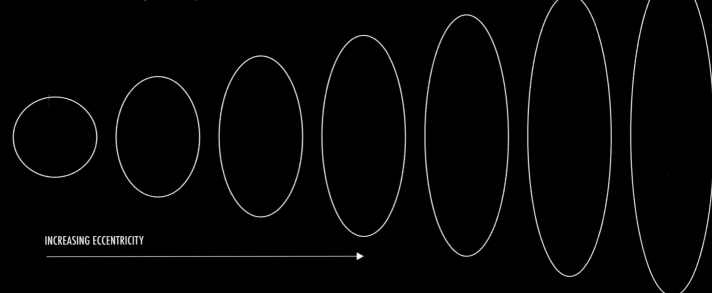

INCREASING ECCENTRICITY

Kepler's First Law states that planets orbiting the Sun follow elliptical paths, rather than exact circles as previously thought. A circle is a type of ELLIPSE, and the diagram above shows a series of ellipses, from a circle on the left, stretching into longer ovals. The more stretched out an ellipse is, the more ECCENTRIC it is said to be.

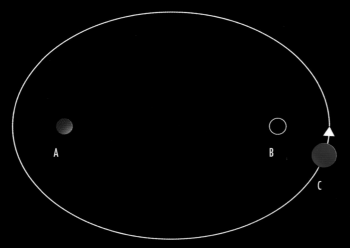

Except for perfect circles, all ellipses have two FOCAL POINTS, or FOCI. Perfect circles have a single focus, in the middle. As ellipses become more eccentric, the foci move closer and closer to the edge.

In the ellipse on the left, the foci are marked A and B.

In planetary orbit systems, the larger body – in this case the Sun – sits at one of the foci, and the smaller body – the Earth (C) in this case – travels around it on an elliptical path.

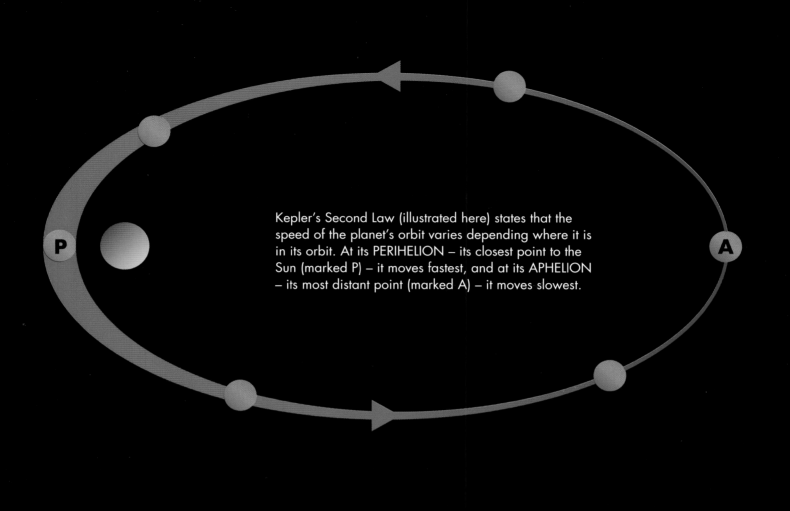

Kepler's Second Law (illustrated here) states that the speed of the planet's orbit varies depending where it is in its orbit. At its PERIHELION – its closest point to the Sun (marked P) – it moves fastest, and at its APHELION – its most distant point (marked A) – it moves slowest.

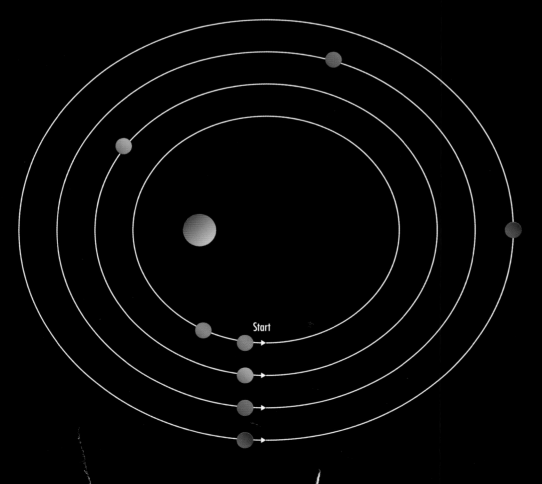

Start

Kepler's Third Law (left) states that the time it takes for a planet to perform one orbital revolution gets greater the further away the planet is from the Sun.

In this diagram, if all the planets begin their orbit at the point marked 'Start', the innermost orbiting planet will have almost finished its orbit while the outermost will have only travelled a quarter of its full orbit.

For example, the Earth takes 1 year to orbit the Sun. In comparison, Neptune, which is much more distant, takes 164 years to complete its orbit around the Sun.

PULSAR
A type of rotating neutron star which emits high-energy electromagnetic radiation. This is picked up on Earth as extremely regular pulses.

RADIATION ZONE
The layer within the Sun between the core and the tachocline in which energy is transmitted via radiation.

RED GIANT
A late-stage star which has inflated to a very large diameter.

REFRACTING TELESCOPE
A telescope which uses the refraction effects of light to magnify distant objects.

ROGUE PLANETS
Planets which do not orbit stars, but instead the centre of the local galaxy.

SATELLITE BUS
A generic system which is used as a framework to create inexpensive satellites.

SCHWARZCHILD RADIUS
The distance between the singularity and event horizon of a black hole.

SINGULARITY
The point of maximum density at the very centre of a black hole.

SOLAR PROMINENCE
An explosion of dense plasma from the Sun's photosphere.

SOLAR WIND
The stream of particles released from the Sun's corona out into space.

SPACE RACE
The competition for dominance in space science between the USA and Soviet Union during the mid 20th century.

SPIRAL ARMS
The curved structures that make up the shape of galaxies such as our Milky Way.

STARQUAKES
Very high energy releases produced by magnetars.

STATIONKEEPING
The act of maintaining the position of a satellite in orbit.

STELLAR BLACK HOLE
A black hole formed from the collapse of a massive star.

STELLAR WOBBLE
A method used to determine the position of exoplanets by the wobble effect their gravity has on the movement of the star around which they orbit.

SUNSPOT
A dark patch on the Sun's surface, caused by lowered temperature as a result of localised magnetic forces.

SUPERMASSIVE BLACK HOLE
A very large black hole formed by the merging of lower mass black holes and other matter. They typically occupy positions in the centre of galaxies.

TACHOCLINE
The boundary between the radiation and convection zones within stars like the Sun.

VAN ALLEN BELTS
Areas of high energy particles held in position around planets by their magnetic fields.

WHITE DWARF
A small dense celestial body formed from the remaining core of a dead star. The light emitted comes from the release of stored heat energy.